Dr Jane Fynes-Clinton has been a newspaper and magazine journalist for more than 30 years. For 15 of those, she has written a weekly op-ed column for News Corp Australia.

Jane was awarded a PhD for a thesis on political communication and lectures in journalism at the University of the Sunshine Coast in Queensland. She is also a regular news and current affairs commentator on radio and TV.

She loves animals, plants and people, a nourishing conversation, a vigorous debate, surfing, running and making a life with her beloved in their home near the ocean.

To Edwin, who gave up countless hours of his precious time and laid himself bare in the telling of his extraordinary life story, I thank you for trusting me. Your clarity, ferocity and strength in life are equalled only by your passion for justice and helping animals. The world is a little better because of you.

To those who supported me and offered warm words of love while I was in the tunnel writing. You made the journey less lonely and reminded me I would eventually get there. My particular thanks to Marleen Groot, who was my travel companion at the beginning and end; and to Michele Gilchrist, who threw me a lifeline by lending me her laptop when mine inconveniently carked it.

To the staff and volunteers at Wildlife Friends Foundation Thailand: my admiration for the meaningful, difficult work you do in very tough conditions. Particular thanks to those who became my friends: Tommy, Aon, Pin, Shawn, Dave and Elliot. I admire who you are and what you do.

Jane Fynes-Clinton

A WILD LIFE: THE EDWIN WIEK STORY

AUSTIN MACAULEY PUBLISHERS™
LONDON • CAMBRIDGE • NEW YORK • SHARJAH

Copyright © Jane Fynes-Clinton (2019)

The right of Jane Fynes-Clinton to be identified as author of this work has been asserted by her in accordance with section 77 and 78 of the Copyright, Designs and Patents Act 1988.

All rights reserved. No part of this publication may be reproduced, stored in a retrieval system, or transmitted in any form or by any means, electronic, mechanical, photocopying, recording, or otherwise, without the prior permission of the publishers.

Any person who commits any unauthorised act in relation to this publication may be liable to criminal prosecution and civil claims for damages.

A CIP catalogue record for this title is available from the British Library.

ISBN 9781528926461 (Paperback)
ISBN 9781528964692 (ePub e-book)

www.austinmacauley.com

First Published (2019)
Austin Macauley Publishers Ltd
25 Canada Square
Canary Wharf
London
E14 5LQ

To those who see the importance, beauty and wonder in living things and who speak up for them.

Author's Note

While there are many angles on any interesting life, this is largely Edwin's version of events. Every effort has been made to cross check verifiable facts, and my own observations gleaned during my half-a-dozen trips to Thailand while working on this book are woven in.

Finally, a note on the chapter titles: Edwin is passionate about 1980s and 1990s' music and film. It seemed only fitting that his life story be punctuated with song titles from that era. They are distinct and enduring – like him.

1. Love Is a Battlefield

Edwin Wiek seems incongruously buoyant today, his short, blond hair neatly combed back and his eyes sharp. Confidence oozes from his stride as he moves towards the Petchaburi Provincial Court building in central Thailand, ready to hear the reading of the appeal decision of the Thailand Supreme Court.

His future is on the line; his work is under judgment. And still, his head is high, and he keeps his gaze steadily on the doors he must pass through. The glass sentinels, the dividing line between his past and future, are standing tall as if to guard the liminal space between what was and what is to come.

This decision is crucial as a finding against him would have smoke-like effects, drifting and reaching and poisoning everything good he has built in the past 17 years. Edwin, Dutch by birth but Thai in life, is a rescuer of wildlife on a grand scale. His Wildlife Friends Foundation Thailand operation is arguably the largest multi-species rescue centre in Asia, and his international reputation as a tenacious agitator for national and international wildlife law reform is formidable. His work has been lauded, awarded and mimicked.

And now the animal activist and wildlife saviour stands accused of the very thing he has dedicated his life to fighting against: illegal wildlife possession.

In 2012, the government cast this vigilante as the villain. They also charged his wife and cast his foundation as sinister, illegal animal law violators. The intent, it seems, was to make him hurt, cause his reputation harm and perhaps, ideally, break him and close his Foundation down.

It came down to paperwork and process, systems and sign-offs. The animals in his care were never pets, never vessels to earn money from or trade in the shifty half-light of the black market. But that is the implication of the offences he was charged with.

Since being hauled into battle, Edwin has ridden the legal waves. He was initially found guilty of illegal wildlife possession, but that decision was overturned on his appeal. Then the prosecution challenged that, and their weaving of a tangled web of paperwork meant the process was stretched out, keeping him awake at night and soaking up thought, time and money – lots of money. Edwin spent 1.5 million baht on legal fees for the fight. It has also taken a massive toll on his work, his relationships, and his physical and mental health.

But today, he is a balanced mix of quiet confidence and being ready to face even the worst of what might come.

He leads the way, striding in his sharp black Wildlife Friends Foundation Thailand polo shirt and green cargo pants. The courthouse's metal detector beeps as Edwin's posse – including the long, angular deputy director of WFFT, Englishman Tommy Taylor – passes into the building, but the security guard does not flinch, much less check bags and bodies. In Thailand, prescribed laws are not always enforced and, on occasion and seemingly at whim, enforcement and legal posturing may rule in spaces where none officially exist. It can feel like an alternative world where the rules shapeshift and authoritarian enforcers evaporate or materialise apparently without reason or rhythm.

Edwin's physical characteristics mean he would stand out anywhere, but in the Thai court building, he is a tall, pink and white beacon and one of only a few European faces. Despite being the dry season, it is steamy in the corridor of the old, slightly unkempt structure. It is a labyrinth with courtrooms and offices not always being consecutively numbered. There is an extraordinary lack of emotion on display amongst the people in the hallways given the seriousness of the core business here, where great slabs of liberty are taken with a word and lives can be snuffed out with a signature.

The hearing is scheduled to start at 9 am, but as is the way of things in Thailand, the court is already running late and proceedings do not get underway until just before 10 am. On this morning's list of decisions and sentences are weapons charges, murder, traffic violations and fraud. Edwin's case is sandwiched after a dangerous driving causing death sentence and before a hearing in a theft case.

The courtroom feels more like a formal office, with stacks of paper on desks at the front. Three rows of pews buffer each side of a centre aisle, a squishy space for defendants and their families to face the music played in Court Room 11. The melody is mostly less gentle symphony and more jarring heavy metal.

Each bench seat would comfortably accommodate four people, but most groan under the weight of five or six, sitting tightly and nervously cheek-to-cheek. Defendants stand where they are, rather than move to a dock to hear their court-determined fate.

Predictably, for one so confident and forthright, Edwin takes a seat in the front row. His lawyer, who has travelled from Chang Mai, wears the standard official attorney's garb of a black robe with short gold sash on the left shoulder and is nearby. Edwin's wife, Jansaeng Sanganork – Noi to anyone who knows her – sits in the pew behind Edwin, her brow knitted as she works her fingers anxiously. Noi has borne the extraordinary weight of these proceedings that have dragged for five years. Her demeanour is sharper than before they began; her health has suffered. She wears the strain on her classically beautiful face. The chief of the village near the Foundation's wildlife rescue centre has come along as a sign of support for Edwin, Noi and the Foundation.

The Supreme Court decision is in a sealed envelope, a white rectangle that holds futures in its folds, that has been transported from Bangkok and is to be opened in front of the defendants to ensure transparency. Edwin stands absolutely erect with his large hands behind his back and his blue-eyed gaze fixed steadily ahead.

The judgment is read out in Thai, sounding to the untrained ear like a peppering of gunfire; the nasal, undulating sound of the Thai language giving no hint at the words' meaning, or whether Edwin and his work can move on or must come to a full stop.

The court's finding is overwhelmingly good; the prosecution's appeal against the not guilty finding is dismissed and Edwin, Noi and the Foundation are cleared of criminal wrongdoing in relation to keeping wildlife. They are free to continue their work. Their names have been cleared. The sad, difficult and damaging saga is over.

But the defendants are criticised for not following procedure on the keeping of paperwork on the animals and are fined the minimum available penalty of 20,000 baht each. It is a face-saving, administrative measure, but a slap in the face none-the-less. Edwin shakes his head, later saying this seems highly unfair given there are no procedural guidelines in place for such bookkeeping under Thai law, and if there are no formal rules, they can't be broken. Edwin's hatred for unfairness almost parallels his loathing of injustice.

Edwin and Noi are taken downstairs and slotted separately in crowded, gender-delineated cells while the paperwork is processed. The worn, barred metal door briefly closes behind Edwin, and he is among murderers, drug dealers and, incredibly, wildlife traffickers. About 25 stressed men squeeze into a cell of about 4x4 metres.

Edwin has been held in jail several times in his life before, but it still prickles him and jangles his nerves. The smell, the feel and the bewildered and fearful faces inside are always the same. The feeling of aloneness and disempowerment are as hollow now as they were when he was first interred in a cell at age 15. The fire that ignites in him in response is primal and raw.

Tommy waits in the dilapidated open courtyard facing the cell, watching anxiously to catch sight of Edwin's white-blond head among the pitch-black ones behind the bars. A slow drip from the air-conditioning unit above dribbles from the gutterless roof and spills onto the broken concrete below. Children eat potato chips and snacks as they play in view of the cells but out of physical or communicable reach of loved ones held within. A heavily tattooed man with 'out of control' emblazoned on his t-shirt is pacing athletically nearby like a wild cat.

Edwin appears from the inky sea and gestures. Nine of the 12 phones available in the courtyard have been ripped roughly from the wall, and Tommy struggles to find a way to talk to his boss. Eventually, they are connected and Edwin talks briefly, steering Tommy to meet him at the finance window once Edwin is extracted from the crowded holding cell. After the fines are paid, Edwin assures Tommy they will be free to go, free to act and free to continue their work.

The relief on Tommy's face is palpable, his dark eyes softening and his handsome features visibly relaxing.

At the end of that day, Edwin, Noi and Tommy have dinner with the staff and 55 resident volunteers at the WFFT rescue centre's communal Elephant Kitchen. By the end of that night, the bottle of Johnnie Walker green label in Edwin's hand is empty, shared in toasting a victory that feels, to him, a little bittersweet and somehow slightly incomplete.

Today, Edwin was at the mercy of the government's legal system. Tomorrow, the wildlife crusader will advise a parliamentary committee on ways to reform the same family of laws that have cast caustic shadows over him for five years.

The irony of it makes him both laugh and cry.

2. Wild, Wild Life

The distinct call of the gibbons is a sign of having arrived at the Wildlife Friends Foundation Thailand rescue centre. There is an occasional undulating movement of the tree branches on petite islands that are dotted on the lake near Khao Luk Chang in the Phetchaburi province of central Thailand, the static canopy set in motion by the long-armed primates at play and in flight.

They sing at dawn and dusk and random times of their choosing in between. The sound is one of joy, archetypally a noise of nature, a brash aural expression of being boldly alive. It is symbolic of everything WFFT stands for: the sound of the wild and the free.

And most saliently, the gibbon islands freedom song emanates from the throats of those once held captive, a vigorous celebration of life from mammals that share the same biological order as those who once hurt them, but now help.

This is ground zero of what Edwin has worked for, fought for, faced charges for and lived for.

The WFFT rescue centre and wildlife hospital complex is opposite the gibbon islands, across a dirt road that skirts the lake's edge, a cluster of low-lying buildings behind a chain-link fence that form the centre's organisational and functional heartbeat. The basic structures are places of administration, shelter, equipment and food storage. Some of the trained staff and all of the myriad international volunteers eat, wash and rest work-weary heads there. Within the conglomeration, the veterinary surgeons and nurses repair broken animal bodies and save lives. Sick and newly-repaired creatures are nursed and tended to.

Their frames might be put back together in the buildings, but the spirits of those captive wild animals are restored away from the concrete and tin. A series of pens, cages and enclosures fan out, offering sanctuary to more than 700 rescued animals, meeting their species-specific needs as much as possible. The process is often slow, spanning years if an animal is particularly compromised. But where there is a breath of hope, they are rehabilitated with the intent of them living out their days in safety and as close to nature as possible. A lucky few – including some of the gibbon groups – are eventually released into the wild.

The gibbons on the islands are in the final stage of the long road to freedom. The release is graduated as the animals often start their days at WFFT so shaped by human interaction they are scarcely aware they are gibbons at all. Some come dressed in human clothes. Many have only ever consumed processed, packaged human food. Several have been so confined that they have lost their ability to sing. Regaining a sense of self and species is a patient, gradual process. Many never make it to what should have always been home, but all are kept safe from human harm and offered a chance to live lives that are as wild as is feasible.

WFFT has several divisions. They include the wildlife rescue centre, which houses the animals that need safe haven and care; the wildlife hospital, which is the best equipped facility of its kind in Asia and includes a full operating theatre, an endoscopy device to allow for less-invasive keyhole surgery and equipment for full blood analysis; the elephant sanctuary; gibbon rehabilitation project and a forest rehabilitation project. There are about 60 employed staff members to help the whole operation run.

Within the wildlife rescue centre's 70ha perimeter fences, the resident animal population is a smorgasbord of diversity. A massive, colourful cassowary, native to northern Australia and southern Papua New Guinea who presumably entered Thailand as a smuggled egg and ended up in WFFT's care after brain-damaging beatings for his instinctive bird behaviours, lives near colourful birds native to Central and South America. Otters frolic in a purpose-built enclosure that includes a water fountain and slide across from a cobbled-together family of Malayan sun bears, who roam and forage in a generous green expanse, and there are Thai animals in their hundreds.

For Edwin, the enormous-and-still-growing WFFT centre at Khao Luk Chang is a dream come true – literally. He is heard often to apologise for sounding cheesy but says the trite maxim must have been rooted in a real experience before it became shop-worn, because he has lived it himself.

"The only difference between a dream and a target is the existence of a plan: I live by that," he says. "You must believe in yourself and you need a lot of luck as well, of course. But if you can channel that drive and can show it to others, you will eventually have other people join you. And that is what I have achieved. That is what I think of when I walk these grounds and feel the satisfaction and deeply warm feeling that comes from watching animals unstressed, at play and interacting as they would in the wild."

Join him, people have.

More than 1500 people aged between 18 and 75 each year come from all over the world to volunteer for a minimum of a week in caring for the animals WFFT has rescued. Most volunteers are in their 20s and from Western nations, and while most stay a week or two, some stay for months, and they all pay for the privilege. Accommodated in basic shared rooms, most shed the decorative vestiges of their regular lives on day one when the oppressive Thai humidity, the egalitarian nature of the physical work and the wonder of being up close with an extraordinarily diverse range of wildlife – and being able to do some real, small thing to help the creatures – settle in.

It matters not if a volunteer is an affluent doctor, intellectual engineer or a youth on a gap year, so life-changing and satisfying is the experience that a high proportion will come more than once. It is hot, tough and physically and emotionally challenging as they work in teams to rake up excrement, scrub pools, prepare copious amounts of food and develop activities that will enrich and enhance the mostly-damaged animals' daily existence. Many of the animals have heart-breaking backstories and difficult behaviours that are the remnants of damage done at human hands either through beatings and neglect or by humanising them to the point of near-death. In those cases, cruelty comes in the form of 'loving' them too much.

The volunteers get up close with these creatures, and that presents its own challenges. It is human to want lavish attention and affection on those down on their luck. But that is not the intent at this special kind of refuge.

The ragtag workforce keeps the place afloat: volunteer payments for what many deem to be a dirty, sweaty privilege, if not at least a life-enriching experience, provide about 70 per cent of the running costs of the Foundation. The biggest drawcard of WFFT is its elephants, the only creatures on the campus to have had their freedom bought. Rescued from tourist-driven trekking camps across Thailand with solid negotiation and the parting of cash, the old ladies carry niggly old injuries and habits from years of being overloaded with tourists on giant baskets that place profit per ride over comfort and health for the beast. Their individual quirks, enormity, wise eyes and road-map skin are magnetic and mesmerising.

All of the elephants have had their spirits dramatically, cruelly broken in their early years to make them comply with their mahout's orders to walk or stay. Some have walked the endless circle for tourist pleasure for 50 years before they came to WFFT. All have spent their lives in chains. But while they may be in their twilight years, here they are given a taste of choice, of being unshackled, of walking free in a forest. And this draws people to want to be near them, to be part of their freedom.

The elephants are partly hands-on in the centre. Volunteers wash them, walk them and feed them. Such is humanity's fascination with these giant mammals that in increasing number of day trippers also pay to have their lives touched by one for a spell. At WFFT, the elephants are not about conservation, because there is no breeding program, and they are never going to be released into the wild. The WFFT responsibility is one simply of providing welfare and wellbeing for the rest of their days.

Edwin says the elephant component of the animal population at the centre started out as a kind of altruistic accident.

"The Wildlife Friends Foundation started as a rescue centre for wildlife, but then an owner of elephants, and I came to an arrangement that enabled them to stay with me for a while," Edwin says. "I basically rented them. I had started looking around at what were called elephant sanctuaries, and I saw they were making a lot of money, and I realised they were not real sanctuaries and that a proper sanctuary could be sustainable and that with the other wildlife I would never be able to grow the income.

"I knew I could do it well – that I could keep true to my initial ethic of the animal welfare and conservation being the focus of the centre – and rescue elephants, which would also bring people. Now, the elephant sanctuary component pays for the wildlife rescue centre. It built the hospital; it pays for my veterinarians. It pays for medication and the cars. The wildlife rescue centre loses money. I can only run the rescue centre because of the elephants. I never lose sight of that."

Edwin says the daily care of animals rescued from domesticity or who are used for entertainment would always remain core business for WFFT. The act of physically removing an animal from a place where it might be being treated as a child or abused – both are equally abhorrent circumstances in the WFFT philosophy – and giving it a chance to live a life that is natural to its species still gives Edwin a natural high.

"Ideally, the best outcome is that you can release an animal back to the wild, but, of course, that is not always possible and even when you do, you know they may not make it," Edwin says. "Habitat loss and poachers are just two of the many threats. But you give them your best – that is the best you can do. And I have always felt that living wild for two years and dying is better than endlessly living as a human captive or slave every day of your life."

Finding out that an animal is in need of rescue, and where it is, can be as challenging as talking the owner into giving it up to the Foundation. A key plank in Thai culture is people minding their own business, even to the extent of not intervening in others' acts of cruelty towards people, animals or property. There are few social controls in Thailand as they exist in European or other Western nations. Traditionally, a person might know that someone close is keeping an animal illegally or not attending to its welfare, but they would most likely consider it none of their concern, even if the animal was suffering.

"It is the same with domestic abuse," Edwin says. "A man can beat his wife and no one will intervene. It happened to me in Cha-Am once when a man was smashing a woman's face into a plate and no one was doing a thing. I spoke up and I had to do a runner because he told me he was going to leave and get a gun.

"Simply, you do not fuck around in other people's business. You don't do that. It is not the Thai way."

With this in mind, WFFT's approach to responding to a call to rescue an animal is with a focus on the animal, not the owner. Edwin has suffered criticism for this from some animal lovers who believe outrage and anger towards those who treat animals cruelly is a fire that must burn brightly, but it was a shift he had to consciously make in his approach for sustainability and also self-preservation.

"In the first couple of years, when I was younger and less experienced, I would get that anger, and I would tell people 'how the hell can you keep this beautiful animal for 10 years in these conditions? Are you stupid?' but that does not get us very far," he says. "The police are not going to start a case, particularly if the animal is from a species that is not endangered, and if I start the process and make a complaint, the police will not help me again because I have made a lot of work for them.

"It also broke me up every time I went out to a rescue, and you can't afford to have your heart broken every day of your life. It is paralysing and pointless. I had to harden up enough that I wasn't constantly upset or angry."

In other ways too, Edwin, a naturally fiery, bold personality, has learnt that he often gets further with honey than with vinegar. Building and maintaining the right relationships has been important to the growth of WFFT, both as a Foundation and a rescue centre.

Most of the staff live nearby, and the centre could not have been built if not for Edwin's close alliance with the local Buddhist temple. He treasures the relationship with the abbot of Wat Khao Luk Chang, who loaned him the initial land on which to build the first enclosures in 2001. The temple monks remains staunchly on his team of supporters, even during times when Edwin has been challenged and criticised by the government, and sometimes the Thai people themselves, for placing such high value on wild lives.

Although Edwin has lived in Thailand for almost three decades – more than half of his life – and can read, write and speak like one Thai-born, he remains both within and without. In many ways, he likes that.

"No matter what, if I did not deeply love it, I would not be here. But I am an outsider, a foreigner," he says. "With strangers who are Thai, I always walk in as someone who is not one of them, but I speak the language, and I know the culture. I offer them respect, and I fit in with how they do things and their cultural behaviour. That is very important. I speak as little English or Dutch as possible in places where everyone else speaks Thai."

Edwin says he will always be Dutch at his core, and he honours his roots, but now he is something of a hybrid.

"I think if I had to explain it, I am half Thai and half Dutch. I am not a Dutchman living abroad: to me, I am home," he says. "I will always be a *farang* – the Thai word for foreigner – in Thailand, but our relationship has matured, like a human relationship does. I am realistic. I am wiser. I know how it works. Let's just say we are no longer in the honeymoon period."

But in the beginning, there was a whole world for Edwin to learn about.

3. Against All Odds

Even at a glance, Edwin is clearly European. His fine blond hair and long lashes, his pale blue eyes and his confident, upright posture scream Dutchman. He has the air that many perceive as arrogance, the direct brashness and a clear, commanding, slightly high voice that demands attention.

Born into a proud Dutch family on December 8, 1965, his early years were a life of comfort and calm. His mother Dymphna was always an elegant, beautiful woman, and his father Eduard was a handsome, charming man. The couple was very young, barely in their 20s, when Edwin's arrival heralded the start of their family.

Eduard had been a soldier for a time, but Edwin's early memories were of admiring his father, a man whose hard and successful work in sales brought the family some of the nice things in life. Eduard drove a beautiful two-door sports car, an Opel Commodore, and ensured that his family wanted for little. Eduard was ambitious, entrepreneurial and took chances with his career moves, displaying a daring that nearly always paid off. The family was cohesive and relatively affluent.

In the early years, Eduard was a copy machine salesman for Gestetner, a revolutionary and important communication development in the 1960s, and moved his family to consecutively larger homes in Den Bosch in the southern Netherlands, before eventually taking up residence on a farm that had a separate office and a spacious house. In time, he started working for himself. In business, Dymphna's need for order and Eduard's entrepreneurial eye were a solid, successful combination.

"My mother was essential to the business: a good salesman is not often a good manager. Good salesmen are like artists – they are creative and good with people, but they are not necessarily good at running things – and my father was one of them," Edwin says.

The entrepreneur branched out. Eduard started with selling delicate silver necklaces emblazoned with names in pretty, cursive fonts, a decorative item that were to become very popular and fashionable in the 1970s. He later expanded his lines, branching into dealing in watches.

Eventually, Eduard opened fashion accessory and jewellery shops, and Edwin worked there on the holidays and at the weekends would sometimes help to repair watches for pocket money. At Christmas time, the shops were heaving with people.

But as the curtain came down on Edwin's childhood, the idyllic notion of family was irreparably torn apart.

When Edwin was in the second year of secondary school, his parents separated in a rather dramatic fashion. In the days before Christmas when Edwin had just turned 13, together they told him that his father was leaving. Edwin can still feel the reverberations of his mother's utter devastation and her rivers of tears in the days and weeks that followed, and he still recalls the cold, bereft sense deep within that comes with feeling the sudden hollowness of what he thought was a happy home. The most difficult part for Edwin was being unable to help his mother feel better or to ease her suffering.

"I had never thought much about parents being separated and I felt very strange about it, like I was the only one," he says. "But then I got back to school after the Christmas and New Year break, I talked to a friend, Kitty, and she told me her parents were divorced too. I realised I was one of a group. I had thought that divorce was rare, but once I started asking, I found almost a quarter of the kids in my class had divorced parents. Others had had a parent die, and I had no real idea that families took all different shapes until that moment. Suddenly, I realised that warm and cosy bonds in families were not something to be taken for granted; that it was very common to have problems."

Edwin later learnt that his father had left the family for someone new, and the other woman was very, very young. His mother had found a rental contract for a home in Antwerp that predated his leaving her, offering documentary proof that he had planned his escape long before Christmas. This brought fresh waves of pain.

"To put it in context, this girl was five or six years older than me. My father was 36. I can understand that he fell for that girl because she was very pretty, and my mother was probably not always easy. But is it worth it to split a family for someone he stayed with for a couple of years? He moved on, and he has since moved on a lot, and I don't think he has ever found that real love he is presumably looking for."

Edwin says his relationship with his father has since been rocky. He sees his father now as ungenerous and lacking in the ability to express real emotion. Now, at 75, Eduard only ever visits his son when his money is tight and his material needs are unmet.

"He bores the shit out of me, to be honest, and he goes on his way when I give him some money. It is his way," Edwin says. "The reason I am not a father now is that I am so worried that I would one day walk away from a wife and child. I do not want to risk doing that to a child. I am not willing to take on that responsibility with a child.

"You need a permit to have a dog, you need a permit to go fishing, but anyone can have a kid. I have always said this and, it is true."

In his early teenage years, Edwin's feelings of helplessness and upset over his parents' separation turned into rage. Feeling somehow responsible, a common response in children, added layers to his emotional turmoil. The times of having his own horses and rabbits, of not wanting for anything material were over. Edwin and his brother, Jurgen, moved into a small home with their mother, and the family home was sold. They suddenly found themselves in an average house in an average neighbourhood, and this was a shock to the boys. While Edwin double-dipped on pocket money, receiving it from both parents, nothing felt as happy as it had once been.

He started to unravel, to disengage and to disrupt. While he started high school in a school for bright students, a gymnasium Athenaeum, the most academic of the school streams, he began to slide and distance himself from learning and the order and discipline required in such a school.

"I was more on the streets with the kids I met in our new neighbourhood than at home or school," he says. "We had come from a farm upcountry to Breda, a medium-sized city. The change was enormous. My new friends and I became a bit of a gang, and I was one of the main instigators of it, always looking for trouble and almost always finding it."

Edwin became involved in petty crime. The group would steal bread from the bakery in the morning, and he would steal metal or wire for his homemade transceivers and satellite dishes. He once stole a radio receiver from a police car in Breda, modified it and took great delight in disturbing the police frequency. Break and enters, petty thefts, causing mayhem and disturbance were all part of the group's modus operandi.

"We told ourselves we were misfits, that we had no chance of fitting into society," Edwin says. "We eventually came across an empty commercial building and took possession of it. We made it ours; it was our clubhouse. We protected it against the police, fighting them when they raided it looking for illegal goods or trying to remove us. We had a loose membership of perhaps 100 people – a huge group – many of whom were much older. Our position was that we might have been misfits but at least we had each other."

By the age of 14, Edwin says nights became a blur of drinking alcohol and smoking marijuana. He acquired a motorbike, and he found new freedom and bigger trouble.

"I was basically lost," he says. "I really did not care about anything – myself, my family, other people's property. I was loose and lost in every way."

The boyfriend of Edwin's mother called the police after a particularly difficult exchange with Edwin, thinking it was the only way to bring him back on track. By this time, Edwin had been enrolled in four high schools and kicked out from three of them. With the latest round of police involvement and subsequent charges, the fourth one had had enough too and excluded him.

He was deemed by the courts to be a delinquent, to be beyond the control of his parents or the law. The judge in his case ordered him to be placed in a boarding school for difficult boys in the east, near the German border. The school was run by Catholic nuns and priests within the Leo Foundation.

"It felt like a jail to me," Edwin says. "I ran away a few times, but they always brought me back. Sometimes, I got quite a long way, up to 150km. Once I called my mother from the village of

Oss to say I was on my way back home, and she called the police to pick me up. I was put in a police cell, and they gave me paper sheets, took the belt out of my pants and put me on suicide watch. The next day, I was taken back to school. Twenty-four hours later, I ran away again."

A suicide at the school was to be a start of a series of events that would end Edwin's reckless, wayward cycle. A very troubled and unhappy boy in Edwin's social group talked a lot about the strictures of his religious family and its difficulties.

"He was questioning everything including his sexuality, and it was very difficult for him," Edwin says. "When the boy said one night that he felt like ending his life, one of the group leaders, presumably without thinking and probably as a kind of strange joke, suggested where he might find a rope.

"He got that rope, and he hanged himself on the top floor of the building. We found him the next day. I was there; I saw him dead, hanging there. When you see that and you are 15, it is very shocking."

Not long after, Edwin himself was brought to the brink, feeling he had no future or hope. He says the shock of his own thoughts and actions jolted him, and he now knows that he never really intended to die, but was simply trying to find a way out or for someone to pay attention in the way he needed it.

"I felt quite hopeless, that there was nothing ahead for me; that I had nothing to give and no value to anyone or anything; that I was never going to have anything to be or do. It was the lowest point in my life, but I also felt shocked at myself. In the moment when I was at my lowest, where I wanted to die, I also felt the fight to survive. It was contradictory: I felt I wanted to die, but I also wanted to live."

The boy's suicide and Edwin's own suicidal thoughts were to bring about a life-altering change. Eduard and Dymphna were so alarmed and concerned about Edwin's welfare that they stepped in and worked with the courts to get Edwin removed from the school and placed in a public high school in Breda.

"My mother found a school that would take me, and I went to this school with my mother and father. The director of the school, a man I only ever knew as Mr Brink, met with us. He was an older man, and he listened to what everyone had to say and at the end, he said 'I want to give you a chance. Nobody else wants you, but I want you in my school. You still have two years to go, and if you come here, I think it will work out. I hope you will do your best.' I will never forget it."

Edwin developed an attachment to both Mr Brink and a man who was the school janitor and handyman, connections that he says made him feel compelled not to disappoint them, even though he still had no issues with disappointing himself. However, he continued not to take his schoolwork overly seriously, he made a lot of jokes and says he was naughty and cheeky.

He was tossed out of the class once for asking at the start of a sex education lesson delivered by a pretty external provider whether the lesson was to be theoretical or practical. In support of a teachers' strike, he put superglue in all the locks of the school including the alarm system. But ultimately, his transgressions were that of a rascal rather than a reprobate and he did not want to let down Mr Brink.

"I realised I had to change," he says. "I did not want to go back to that other school. One of my friends went to jail at 18 for two years, and I did not want that for myself. I was an adult at 15 because I had an adult awareness of what was going on at 15.

"On reflection, I know I did not have a childhood from the time my parents separated. My brother was younger and was not as strong as I was, and I stepped up to being an adult then, without knowing how to be one. But at this high school, now I knew. Now I realised I had to get myself together."

That Mr Brink invested faith in him was the first time Edwin deeply comprehended the notion of second chances, and it was a faith and action that he was to take with him into adulthood.

"It affected me. It made me realise that you are not done for or destined because of what has happened to you or the circumstances that you have created," he says. "Against all odds, he gave me a second chance where no one else would. And for that reason, I respected and loved him in a way.

"My life and my work now is about giving animals a second chance and that came from the deep experience and knowing I had via Mr Brink at 15. Second chances are so important."

By the time Edwin finished high school, he was among the highest academic achievers in his cohort. Mr Brink came up in those last days, gave him a hug and said 'I knew you could do it.

I am so happy you did because I can now tell people you were worth it and other people in your position are too'. Edwin says it was an exchange he will never forget and revisits in his dreams.

At 17, Edwin was deposited into the world.

Still officially under the care and control of the courts, he was compelled to appear before a juvenile court judge. He was required to give an account of what his post-school plans were. An assessment by social workers was also made on his state of mind and behaviour.

"They are the kind of people with beards; the women had unwashed hair and were all soppy and saying they were going to take care of you. What bullshit. They think they know better because they have studied. They are the Leftish kind of people I still despise. I hate them; I still can't stand them; for me, self-righteousness is almost as ugly as jealousy.

"My father used to say that if a man is not on the Left when he is young, he has no heart. If he is not on the Right as he grows, he has no brains. I think that is very true because you have to be compassionate, but also practical and pragmatic."

Marooned with no real life plan, Edwin suggested to the child court judge, Mr van der Goes van Naters, that he might have some sort of gap year to work out his next steps, but the child guardian deemed that a year of unstructured time would be destructive for a boy with Edwin's troubled record.

"Mr van der Goes van Naters told me I was going to choose work or study, or he would make the decision for me," Edwin says. "A few weeks later, I got a letter giving me a time and date for a physical and mental check to precede my entry to the army. Of course, at that first check I did my best to show that I was crazy and thought I had been quite successful at that.

"I was hoping to be found unfit for army service, but I got a letter asking me to come back in. I was a bit shocked. The man on that second check said 'you are very fit. You could do anything in the army'. I said I thought I was a misfit, a bit crazy. But he said 'you are fine, you will fit right in. See you when you are 19.'"

In 1983, young men in The Netherlands did national service at 19: 14 to 16 months of armed services training. The practice was suspended in 1996.

But rather than wait, Edwin was to be fast tracked. The court contacted Edwin at the end of that summer, asking for evidence of whether he was working or studying. At the time, Edwin's father had planned to take him to the south of France for a 10-day holiday, and Edwin vowed to respond to the court on their return.

"During the trip to France, my father would use me with my long blond hair and smile, all nicely dressed up, to hit on women. Girls would come to speak to me, and I would talk to them, and he would smooth things out with drinks and charm. I found all of it to be fun, and my father paid for everything. It was quite a wonderful holiday for me, thinking back.

"We listened to a tape of Dire Straits' *Telegraph Road* album during the whole holiday. It is a soundtrack of that time for me."

When they came back to The Netherlands, there was a letter giving Edwin a date in September to go to a recruitment office to enter the Army.

"I gave in to the idea then, figuring if I did not go now, I would have to at 19, and I might be doing other things by then, and it would interrupt my life. So I thought, *Let's do it*."

Army service cemented many of the life skills Edwin had begun developing in Mr Brink's school.

"In the army, I certainly learnt self-discipline. I learnt in a practical way to problem solve," Edwin says. "I learnt that a problem today can be a solution tomorrow. My boundaries completely changed. I met some guys who became lifelong friends.

"I had already spent time in boarding schools, so I knew what it was to live under one roof, in one room, with other guys. And by now, I was smart enough to know how to stay out of trouble."

Edwin was also taught how to gather intelligence from reliable sources, something that would become very useful later in his life. He sees the time in the army as a kind of twilight zone between segments of his life.

"By the time I came out, I was ready for anything. I had been exposed to harsh conditions and circumstances that required me to step up and get tough. It opened my eyes to being away from the influences of my home region."

On his discharge from the army, Edwin was taken on by one of his father's competitors and friends, Harold Klap, in his fashion accessories business. Edwin went to Arnhem, Belgium, where he was given free residence in an empty warehouse, to protect it from squatters in the lead up to it being fitted out for the business. He moved in with baseball bat in hand. The irony was not lost that only a few years before, he had been a squatter himself. He knew the game well. Edwin began a job in Harold's company, organising packaging and dispatch of the jewellery and accessories.

"After a couple of months, the girls in the company said to Harold 'this Edwin is cute and easy going. He gets along with people'. So Harold took me to this trade fair to help with writing down orders and said at the end that I could be useful in sales. Some people thought I was a bit flirty and a bit charming, so every Monday, I was sent to the trade fairs in Utrecht in the centre of Holland. That grew to being three days in the stock room and two days in the show room, preparing the items for display. Eventually, I started to work on Saturdays and was always the first one in the office and the last one to leave."

After two years, Harold offered Edwin the chance to design some of the accessories. He noted with surprise that Edwin was by then fluent in Dutch, German and English, the accidental result of a natural ear for languages consolidated by his time in the military.

In December 1986, Harold told Edwin he was taking him to the Far East. The thought was exotic to Edwin, he had visions of heat and heady aromas and spiced food. They left separately and met in Seoul, Korea.

"I was stupid then. I thought everything in the Far East was always warm, and I took light-weight clothing. I was an idiot, of course, because Seoul is freezing in December. I got there in my linen pants, my pink short sleeves and pastel blue tie, no jacket, and it was minus 18 degrees Celsius. I immediately went out and bought a *Top Gun*-style flight jacket. The movie had just been released, and they were all the rage at the time. My relative in Thailand was cremated in that jacket in 1991. He loved it. So did I."

On that trip, Edwin and Harold visited South Korea, Hong Kong, Taiwan and The Philippines in 10 days. Edwin was excited by Asian cultural differences and the distinctive customs and practices. The strangeness of the lands invigorated rather than deterred him.

A couple of months later, Harold sent Edwin again to source different lines for the business. He visited the same nations as well as Thailand. The next year, Edwin made seven business trips to Asia, consolidating his affection for the exotic and different ways of living and operating in nations beyond Europe.

By now, his head was in gear, but then his heart was set on fire.

Edwin had already had some girlfriends but never one like Marianne, an actress and model in Indonesia. Her parents were Dutch, but Marianne had grown up in Jakarta and gone to an international school there.

Edwin met this striking beauty at the Arnhem home of his then-girlfriend Anne-Marie. Marianne, a tall, blonde stunner, turning heads wherever she went, was the opposite of his dark-haired then-girlfriend.

She and Edwin became great friends and fell into a comfortable pattern of going places together and having dinner at the home where Edwin lived alone. Edwin's girlfriend was not allowed to go out with him except on Friday and Saturday nights, and even then she had a curfew. Edwin and Marianne would call each other, make food together and sit together on the couch watching TV.

"We even slept together in the same bed, but I never touched her. We were so comfortable. I would look at her for hours, sleeping. I would dream about sleeping with her, but I *was* sleeping with her just not having sex with her.

"I soon realised I was absolutely in love with her. She was certainly the biggest love of my life."

Edwin kept his feelings to himself, not wanting to ruin their friendship and fearing his affections were not returned.

"For some reason, I was always insecure about that. When I was younger, I would not tell a girl I liked her, fearing she would reject me," he says. "Just before Christmas, Marianne was to go back to Jakarta for a holiday. The night before she left, I told her I was going to miss her. She looked at me strangely and asked me to expand on that, 'miss me like a boyfriend misses a girlfriend?'

"I got emotional. I said to her, 'I am so in love with you. I love everything about you, and I have for so long. I feel so upset that you are going.' She sat up, and she turned on the lights in the bedroom and said 'are you crazy?' I said 'about you, yeah, I am'. And then I finally got to kiss her."

The pair was to be awake all night.

"It was the most passionate night I have ever had," Edwin says. "She was amazing; she was so beautiful. And she was leaving."

Marianne's brother came to pick her up to take her to the airport, and she told Edwin their night together had been a one-off that could not be repeated. After all, he was still dating her best friend.

"The moment she got back in the second week of January, she called me and said she might come and see me later that week. I remember thinking 'later this week? I want to see you right now!' She did not know that two days after we slept together, I went to see my girlfriend and told her it was finished with her. I did not tell her about Marianne, but she found out later."

Edwin arranged to have a drink with Marianne that evening and told her that he had broken up with Anne-Marie. Their love blossomed. They were together for two-and-a-half years, a time Edwin recalls as some of the happiest of his life. He had found a love that felt complete in a person who was beautiful, interesting and stimulating. But then a subtle shift, a distance had developed in Marianne, something that Edwin says he could not put his finger on.

Marianne went away for work, so Edwin went out with friends to celebrate Carnival, three days of drinking and partying, and he found himself sharing a bed with a girl who was a friend of a friend.

"We were in a farming area, and I can still remember waking up with the smell of pig shit everywhere," he says. "I still can't get that out of my brain. It was alcohol; it was stupid. I was not even particularly attracted to her, but she offered herself, and I went there."

When Marianne returned, Edwin told her about his one-night stand.

"It was the biggest mistake of my life," he says. "I should never have told her; it did not mean anything. But I know now that it was when she decided to leave me, even though it took her four or five months to finally do that."

In the summer, Marianne took their cat Twit and went to Jakarta, saying she would be back in a month or two. She was working, filming advertisements.

"She did not write or call for six weeks, and I started to realise something was permanently, unchangeably wrong," he says. "I tried to call her, and she would not pick up.

"I decided to call her one day at a time when she would not expect it, on a Wednesday morning, and I got her on the phone. She said she could not talk because her mother was there, but that on the Saturday her parents were going to an embassy party, and she would be free to talk at about eight in the evening. She said she had bad news.

"I knew what was coming, and I had to have her back. I knew that instead of calling her, I had to be there on her doorstep."

Edwin went to Harold and resigned. Knowing Edwin's plan and caring deeply for him, Harold said he could keep the company car, a VW Golf, as a golden handshake. He gave him 10,000 guilders, or about four months' salary, and he paid for Edwin's ticket to Jakarta.

Harold had booked the cheapest ticket he could find, a long way around. Edwin's father drove Edwin to Dusseldorf, in Germany, where he flew to Bangkok and on to Jakarta, arriving on a Saturday morning. He checked into a Jakarta hotel and decided to go and see Marianne as soon as it was dark.

"I rang the bell and her brother opened it and started laughing, saying 'this is going to be fun'. I waited on the footpath, and I heard some stuff in the kitchen flying. Five minutes later, Marianne walked out, and I felt like I was in a movie. She said 'what are you doing here?' and I said 'what do you think I am doing here? I don't think you get it. I love you.' She told me her parents were home. She said she had a new boyfriend, and he was a lawyer from California, and her parents were very happy with him. She said if she went back to me, her mother never wanted to see her again.

"OK, so I got it. I wasn't good enough. It felt like the ground had given way."

Shattered, Edwin told her where he was staying and got in a taxi and went back to his hotel. When he got there, there was a woman in the lobby, Cathy Rubin – the daughter of one of the biggest shoe traders in the United Kingdom. Harold had been in touch with her and asked that they keep an eye on Edwin, worried that he was headed for heartbreak.

She and her companions asked Edwin to go out for a few drinks.

"I was beside myself, but I had not given up on Marianne yet. I just did not know what my next step would be. I never give up that easy," he says.

To drown his sorrows, Edwin went with the group to the piano bar at the Hilton, and through Cathy, Edwin met people from the shoe business. From there, they went to the Jaya pub, a venue frequented by foreigners where there was live music. Given the chance, Edwin was quick to step up the microphone.

"I was heartbroken and drunk, the best recipe for singing," he says. "At that moment, Marianne's father walked in, and shook his head at me. I stopped singing immediately. Behind him was her mother, and behind her was Marianne and her new boyfriend. Unbelievable.

"I looked at her and just felt this deep sadness. She eventually sat at the bar about 20 metres away, and I went over to her and said 'you let me go for this guy? He is a fucking jock.' He looked like a stereotype out of a movie like *Sixteen Candles* or something. I told her she was the love of my life and that I could not help it, that this was all a terrible series of mistakes. She left, upset.

"I felt pulled apart. But my group moved on to the Tunamur, a discotheque I had never been to before that I found out later was also a venue for freelance prostitutes. About 3 am, I got a tap on the shoulder, and it was Marianne, asking what I was doing there. I told her I was just having a drink, and that was the only thing I could think to do. I was very drunk, and she was very angry, so she left."

At 8:30 am he returned to his hotel and checked out. He called Harold, who was working in Manilla, booked a cheap flight to meet him there, and asked for his job back.

"He told me he was willing to have me back, but that he had a call from a contact in England, and he was willing to give me a job too. I would work for Harold and the contact out of Hong Kong as a purchase controller, sourcing products and materials for them both. I considered this, thinking, 'well, in Hong Kong I am at least five or six thousand kilometres closer to Marianne'. She said she had decided she was to be based permanently in Jakarta."

Edwin went back to Holland, emptied his apartment, put all his keepsakes in storage and moved to Hong Kong. He arranged for his mail to be forwarded to his mother's address. It was October 1989.

Edwin did not hear from Marianne. He planned to go home for Christmas, knowing she would possibly do the same, but work kept him in Hong Kong. It was the loneliest Christmas of his life.

A box arrived from Holland from his mother, containing Christmas gifts. Inside was a bunch of letters from Marianne that had arrived in the months before. Edwin assembled them in order of the date stamp.

The first letter told him that on the fateful night in Jakarta, after seeing him drunk, she had decided to defy her mother and had come to his hotel lobby, waiting until 7am for him to return. She presumed that he had gone somewhere with one of the girls in the disco and had returned to her parents' home.

It had all come crumbling down through a series of misunderstandings and wrong steps. Edwin was shattered all over again.

In February, on a trip to report on his work, Edwin went to the office in Arnhem, where Marianne was visiting by coincidence.

"I made an appointment to see her, and we got into my car. We drove to the forest for a quiet place to talk, and I hoped to later find privacy in a hotel room where I could properly communicate my love for her. It was cold, I recall. But we did it right there in the car."

But Marianne had by then moved on, and their lives had moved in different directions. Eventually, they parted permanently. But the die was cast: the only solid thing left in Edwin's life was his new existence in Asia.

4. Hungry like the Wolf

Life in Asia is in equal measure easy and hard for a European, but in the necessary ways, Edwin settled in quickly. This was not a temporary move, and he threw himself into learning the culture, the social mores, and, most of all, the ways of sharply and efficiently running his businesses.

Already multilingual, his steel-trap mind locked onto the tonal tongues of Asia, rapidly learning not only the words, but also the deep and textured ways of the East where the official lines are often in sharp contrast to the accepted common practises. In many ways, Asia was a perfect fit for someone as edgy as Edwin; he had learnt through the hard experiences of rebellion in childhood that success and longevity were more likely if you could operate mostly by the book to start with but be ready to jump if you caught sight of something exciting in the margins.

He built work and personal contacts, crafting a vigorous social life and embracing the wild, colourful life that was on offer to a white man in a Hong Kong that was then still under British rule. They were heady, crazy, hard-working days, and Edwin operated on minimal sleep and with maximum energy. He was socially and professionally stimulated in ways he had not previously experienced. Happily, he found very little was off limits once he had immersed himself in this heaving, colourful land; he just had to find who to know and how to find the crevices and crannies.

At the time, Edwin juggled work for the two fashion accessories and shoe companies, Gronilux BV based in The Netherlands and a subsidiary of Pentland which was based in Leicestershire in the UK. But in early 1990, financial markets shifted and twisted and belt tightening began. This meant that expenditure was reduced and as Dutch and English companies cut costs wherever possible. Edwin felt he could no longer do his job in the ways he had come to embrace. When new management took over the companies he worked for, introducing demands that could not be easily accommodated within the Hong Kong model, Edwin knew it was time to step out on his own.

At the time, Edwin's driving motivation was to make money – and lots of it. He became aware that he had developed the capacity to generate virtually as much money as he desired and he had become accustomed to a life of plenty: hard work and hard play all at a pace that sharpened his senses and got his blood pumping.

Under his companies' employ, Edwin was earning about $US1400 a month, with his apartment paid for in addition. Edwin felt that if he could have $20,000 in orders on the books and take the standard five per cent commission, he would get $1000 a week. Good at selling, he knew this was entirely within his abilities, and this would give him a very good life indeed in Hong Kong.

"Being between a manufacturer and a customer meant you were always a bit squeezed on both sides," he says. "The supplier always wants to sell for a higher price to make money, and the buyer or importer abroad wants it cheaper. In the middle was my commission and while you might get 5 per cent on a small order, you would go down in the percentage with big orders. I soon realised that I could make some of these products myself, which meant I could have the supplier-manufacturer profit as well as my commission. I went out on my own, and that meant I could then control the quality, production and delivery which sometimes were not up to my standards. I found the right sub-contractors, and they eventually became my employees, and I consolidated more of the work in-house."

Even now, Edwin says he is a stickler for quality control in whatever it is he is responsible for, a vestige of that business experience. During the year in Hong Kong, Edwin was also asked to reorganise a production facility for fashion accessories in Cebu, The Philippines. He spent several months helping to reorganise the operation – a personal favour for Harold. Harold's Austrian friend and his Thai wife had 200 employees but had little clue, in Edwin's opinion, about business. Getting the operation on its feet was satisfying for him.

After a year in Hong Kong, Edwin realised it was cheaper to live in Thailand, and he was by now familiar with the subtle differences between the British-Chinese ways of Hong Kong and those in Thailand.

"Thailand was freer. It had a better lifestyle than the city life of Hong Kong," he says. "I could work hard during the week and get on my chopper motorbike and go to the beach at Pattaya or Hua Hin at the weekends. So many things about it were appealing, and it just made sense for me at that time in my life."

He bit the bullet and made the move southwest in April 1990.

He rented an apartment on Sukhumvit Road in the centre of Bangkok for 2500 baht a month and sourced factories capable of producing his desired fashion items. He officially set up European Fashion Accessories and, later, EFA Trading. Through consuming 20 or 30 magazines from Europe each month, he would copy ideas, adapt the trends he saw there, have them made up and export the items to his contacts in Europe. He aimed for the middle of the market, his profits coming out of quantity. Initially, he contracted factories for manufacture, but later he had his own production houses, further increasing his profits.

Later, when the business was on its feet, Edwin would travel to Milan, London, Paris and Frankfurt to gather ideas for designs.

He partied and networked, making friends and settling into a lifestyle that was hard working and hard playing. The nightlife brought him into contact with many Westerners, some of them very successful in banking and business. In some, he found friends. One Canadian man, who spoke fluent Thai and had lots of money to spend every night, he held up as an example of the kind of businessman with a vibrant life that Edwin wanted to emulate. The Canadian was dealing in antique furniture, sourcing colonial pieces and sending the pieces back to US and Canada.

"As he was so fluent in reading and writing Thai and had a lot of money, he was my idol. He disappeared from the bar and club scene somewhere in 1992, and I only found out later he was a drug dealer and had committed suicide after being charged and facing death via a Bangkok prison.

"I realised then that speaking fluent Thai and having lots of money is not always a barometer of success."

In 1992, Edwin moved to Cha-Am purely because it was upcountry and easier to keep staff long-term at a better rate than in Bangkok. Employees were derived from the local area and therefore could stay with their families. The operation was soon bedded down and running well.

"Getting the right staff was challenging. There is an enormous difference between Europe and Asia in work ethic. The right staff are those who will do exactly what you want and turn up to work on time, and that is hard to get in Thailand," he says. "And if you don't pay much money, you get a cheap product; if you pay more, you get better. But you can't change the overall attitude of the people; you can't change what came before you and will stay long after you. You have to work with that and try to capacity-build within."

Edwin reasoned that paying a little above the going rate and offering healthcare as part of the employment package would help build his reputation and make his staff more secure and want to work harder. It worked, and his company was featured in a TV show in Belgium for this initiative so radical it was at the time.

Hair ornaments were very on trend at the time scrunchies and bows and frills, and he produced millions of units a year. The company also made some bags and tops. He secured a small contract with Disney and produced items for a couple of key European fashion houses known for their quality goods, and this brought others in.

"I would always personally approach the people from whom we sourced our raw materials, and I decided who we did business with and who we didn't. I was not inclined always to go for the best price without considering the long-term business relationship. You always must look at the price and quality, but also those who you rely on and their ethics and standards," he says. "This was not because I was particularly compassionate or humanistic: it just made good business sense to me. You should never be too greedy or let money cloud long-term judgement.

"Relationships in business with the right partners are imperative to success. If my suppliers and buyers could make a living from my business, I had a very good chance of having a good supply for good materials, a decent delivery time and smooth transitions every step of the way. This is important because if one of the elements does not work well and in a timely way, my manufacturing stops and my costs continue. Importantly, my income would cease. I was successful with it in ways that I found very satisfying."

Edwin's manufacturing company did not use fur or other animal products. He says it was not a policy; he just did not want to. He says the company was not particularly environmentally conscious, not particularly eco aware. These were not concerns of that era, and he was largely unconcerned with follow-on environmental impact then.

Edwin had made many friends in the Cha-Am community, including a fellow Dutch ex-pat fashion accessories manufacturer Siska Schippers and her partner Willie van der Meijde. Siska's designer handmade jewellery continues to be a growing international business under the label Zsiska.

Willie became a drinking buddy, and in Siska, Edwin discovered a strong shared fascination with the exotic animals in Thailand. Their conversations deepened as they each learnt about the creatures of the forest. Willie did not share Siska's interest, so soon Siska and Edwin began to regularly venture together into Kaeng Krachan National Park on their days off in an effort to see animals in the wild. It was purely fun and a pressure release from their hectic work demands.

"We knew fuck-all about wildlife," Edwin says now. "But we went there quite often, and we developed strong feelings for it and a great interest in the animals and what we saw. There was so much I wanted to know.

"We would see these beautiful animals in the jungle and we did not know what they were, but we loved it; we were really excited by it. Then we would drive back through the villages and see the same species of these wild and free animals chained to a tree or in a cage, and you begin to realise that is not right.

"That is how it started."

Kaeng Krachan is lush, and its hills are undulating, but it is most notable for its wildlife diversity. More than 400 species of birds and 300 butterfly species have been officially recorded there, and it is arguably the pick of Thailand's national parks for bird and butterfly watching. Hidden in the folds of the 2900 square kilometres are also 57 mammal species, who live wild lives, secreting themselves under the rainforest canopy and finding security in the lush land that is built on the map sliced by two mostly-swollen rivers that wend their way to the Gulf of Thailand.

This was where Edwin first saw examples of many of the species that he would later have within his sanctuary.

He was utterly smitten.

Edwin had also settled in his domestic life. He had met Nimuknin Onying at a bar one night, introduced by a Belgian friend who had a Thai girlfriend. Nimuknin, or Noi as she was known, struck Edwin from the first moment.

"She was an absolutely stunning woman to see," Edwin says. "She stood out in the crowd for her beauty. She had class, and she had a lovely body, but the most important thing to me was her face. She was so very pretty, and I love a pretty face more than a beautiful body. She had glossy, long black hair. I was struck by her warm, open face and her beauty."

Noi was informed, well-connected and loads of fun. She was interesting in a way Edwin had not struck in a woman for a long time, challenging him and discussing topics that mattered to Edwin and offering her knowledge gleaned from being from a family that had lived in Thailand for generations, and she was undemanding in their social activities and outings. In many ways, to Edwin she felt like a perfect girl: she gave him freedom to go out with his friends and to work events without her and was keen to help him grow his business. She wanted Edwin's happiness and success most of all.

"I also liked that she did not demand that I should lavish or spoil her then. I had a simple apartment and a motorbike, and she was very happy with that. We made our own fun, and we just got along," he says.

Noi soon became intrinsic to the business, taking over the human resources component and sourcing staff. She and Edwin fell into a rhythm in life and in work, and in the first flush of love, it was mostly the stimulating, satisfying beat that Edwin had always craved. They travelled a little, visiting Egypt, Greece, Czechoslovakia as well as The Netherlands on different trips, and they adventured well together. Edwin's family liked her.

Their joint happiness made them a solid business team and that brought success. Business boomed; they eventually employed more than 200 people, and they gained social status and gathered beautiful things. Edwin has always been a consummate host to those he chooses for company and is generous and charming in conversation. Even in the early years, he liked to share what he had with friends.

Thailand's wild and seemingly contradictory politics were a source of fascination and frustration for Edwin almost from the start. The texture and passion of it still intrigues him, and he has more than once found himself in the engine room, being spattered by the grease and baked by the heat.

Black or Bloody May exploded on Bangkok streets in 1992. General Suchinda Kraprayoon had overthrown the democratically elected but openly corrupt government the year before, and when it seemed the coup was to be legitimised, the people rose up with up to 200,000 people taking to the streets. Edwin had observed the international media had been reporting on the unrest for days, but nothing had been reported in the Thai media.

"I said to Noi, 'the BBC and CNN are talking about these big protests and on Thai TV there is nothing. I want to see it for myself'. So that weekend we decided to go on my Yamaha chopper motorbike into Bangkok's centre, and I told Noi to wear a bright orange shirt because no one wears orange in this country, and she would be easy to see if we got separated. Thai people all have black hair and from the back the women look the same.

"It was crazy; it was wild. The people were surging and pushing, and it was very tense. Suddenly, the authorities started to arrest the leaders of the protest, and they were shooting with machine guns. It was mad and exciting all at once. It was amazing to be on the edge of something so big, so important. I thought this was history: this was going to change everything, and Thailand would be free of a corrupt government."

Edwin and Noi stayed for three or four nights, and Edwin met up with a man who is still a friend, Belgian journalist Mark Hoogsteyns, a long-time war reporter. Always a technophile, Edwin was an early adopter of the mobile phone which at the time was a cumbersome brick-like object. He found himself suddenly in high demand with media outlets asking to use his contraption and, because his English was so good and he was in the thick of the action, talk on air to the big networks in the UK and US. He was paid for regular updates, taking on the role of a kind of circumstantial journalist. Through the viewfinder of his super VHS video camera, he observed and filmed the passion of the seething, angry masses and the power applied as the protest was crushed, recording killings at the hands of the military including one where a man carrying a photo of the royal family was shot through the head.

US journalist Tom Mintier and his soundman overheard Edwin saying he had just caught a killing on tape and paid him $300 cash on the spot. The footage was broadcast internationally.

"I was in the thick of it, and I loved it. There were shootings; I was holed up sometimes overnight hidden in the gutter with gunfire overhead to get the right footage or just to see what was going on. I felt I had to be a part of it, but it was fucking dangerous.

"Noi felt very strongly in support of the demonstrators and was there as well. Of course, in the end, what we call Black May 1992 was all for nothing, and the military remained in power."

The military crackdown resulted in 52 officially confirmed deaths, many disappearances, hundreds of injuries and more than 3500 arrests. Many of those arrested were tortured.

Edwin and Noi moved into a beautiful 115-year-old stately manor house in 1996 across the road from the languid Cha-Am beachfront. It became a haven and a place renowned for gatherings in the ex-pat European community. He felt balanced, if not always utterly settled, and the whisper of agitation for something more began to find its quiet voice within him.

"I could have done anything: I had the means to. But sometimes it did not feel like enough," he says. "But when you make a lot of money and have a lot of staff working for you, of course you feel invincible. You have that bank balance, that beautiful house and that beautiful wife. Everything should have felt perfect. Talking Heads had a song about that."

Most days, he could find some satisfaction at work and play. But in the middle of the beauty, the things and the pace, Edwin began to increasingly wonder if he would ever feel truly satisfied with his life. Then a higher purpose found him in the form of a cheeky monkey.

"A Scottish friend Alan McDonald had bought a monkey for his wife in June 1999, a two-month-old, long-tailed macaque, which I called Kijke; it is Dutch for 'looking'. I don't know why the hell Alan did that in the first place, but that monkey was crying all night, pissing and shitting in the bed, so of course pretty quickly he wanted to get rid of it.

"I had a lot of dogs and cats, and I would pay for the spraying of a lot of street dogs in my area. He said to me, 'you love animals so much, and I have this monkey that is giving me the shits. You will know what to do with it'. I spoke much better Thai than he did, so he asked me to find a home for it. He brought me the monkey, and I thought, *I will keep it; it is cute.* He was a beautiful little baby, and I was quite fascinated by him and how he moved and interacted with me.

"I built a beautiful cage for him and started looking for a place for him to go permanently, but the only government breeding/rescue centre nearby was a shithole at that time. I did not think I had any other option; I was very busy at work and did not have children so having a baby that needed taking care of was not something I wanted for myself right then, so I made an appointment to hand it over at the government centre. That was all for nothing: they said they did not want it."

Realising he was ill-equipped to care for the toddler monkey, Edwin did some research and found a phone number for an organisation called Wild Animal Rescue Foundation. Edwin was brought in touch with the founder of WAR, Leonie Vejjajiva – a well-connected British woman who was married to Pongsak, a relative of the then-future controversial Prime Minister Abhisit Vejjajiva. Leonie was a wildlife lover and, at that time, had 10 or 12 gibbons in her backyard in the middle of Bangkok with an office not far away that had another dozen or so animals in the parking lot of the 20-storey building.

Their first exchange was unpleasant. Down the phone line, Leonie balled Edwin out for having a monkey at home, but when he assured her that he was trying to give the monkey up and had the animal's best interests at heart, she relented and agreed to meet him.

"Alan and I put Kijke in my pick-up truck and said we would go and see their operation, and I thought I would give them a nice donation to build something for Kijke," Edwin says.

"We got there. I saw these beautiful gibbons in her backyard and saw the monkeys in small cages in her parking lot, and I thought, *I don't like this. It doesn't feel right.* I mean, I was not an expert but seeing these wild creatures in such small spaces just felt every kind of wrong. And then we got upstairs, and there was a monkey chained to one of their desks. It was everything I hated and did not want for wild animals.

"I said hello to Leonie, and she was still on her high horse and talking to me like I had done something wrong. It really made me mad, and I told her I was not comfortable giving up Kijke until I knew that he would be living somewhere better than I had made for him.

"She told me she had a wildlife facility at Lopburi, and I told her I wanted to have a look. She backed up a bit then, saying there was no cage yet, but if I would fund one, they would build it. She said she needed 300,000 baht; at the time, I had no idea what these things cost, but I now know that was an excessive amount for what was required."

By now, Edwin was determined to keep caring for Kijke, feeling that even though monkeys are imminently social and Kijke had a growing need for monkey companionship, he would keep learning about macaques and what they needed until he found something better.

"I felt very uncomfortable, very sad that this was better than the government facility, but that if this was the best around, we had failed these animals badly. I remember that feeling inside; it was like a pain in my chest for the monkeys and gibbons," he says. "I asked about the baby monkey chained to the desk, whom they called Jah. Leonie told me he was there because there was no room anywhere and that the cages downstairs were full. I said, 'those cages downstairs are 1x1 metre. That is appalling. You can't keep them like that'.

"I told her that by comparison, I had built a cage quickly for Kijke, and it was 8x4m and four metres high at my house. That was for just one monkey, and I had a pool in there and things for him to play with."

Realising Leonie could be offended, Edwin braced for a fight and told her that while he understood it was important for monkeys not to be alone, he was not willing to give Kijke up until he felt sure his care would be equal to or better than he already had. Far from fighting him, Leonie then asked if Edwin could take Jah with him to his home on the beach in Cha-Am.

"So instead of giving up my one monkey, I left Bangkok with two," he says. "This was not how I thought my day would turn out."

It was a Friday, and the macaque was to be called Friday from that day onwards.

Cute, cheeky and now partners in mischief, Friday and Kijke became intrinsic to the family and the daily routine. Because they cried at night, the babies slept in Edwin's bed with him and Noi. Edwin custom-made diapers to accommodate their tails and save on cleaning.

"In the evenings, before they got tired, they would play in the water in the sink. Long-tailed macaques love water," Edwin says. "They would play until they got tired, then they would cry, and I would towel them off, put them in their Pampers, and they would sleep under my armpits. In the morning, I would feed them, put them in the cage and go to work and we got a maid to take care of them through the day."

Edwin was feeling his way in this new, wild world of animal care, and on reflection, he says he did many things wrong. They were given human toys and taught to interact civilly. While they were given their species-appropriate food, the monkeys loved to eat rice and French fries and Edwin loaded them up – something he says makes him shudder today. They would steal strands of spaghetti from his plate and run with them waving behind like a ribbon around the house. This fun game meant he and Noi stopped having tomato-based sauces because it soiled the walls. Cream sauce, it turns out, is easier to wipe off.

Siska was a regular guest to their home, and it was not the food she came for. Friday, in particular, loved her.

Leonie called a month later, to say the cage was not quite ready, but asked if Edwin could go to a temple at Pa La-u and pick up a gibbon and keep it at his home for a short while before it would be taken to a gibbon rehabilitation project at Phuket.

"I go to the temple and there is this fully-grown gibbon chained to a chair. He was friendly – his name was Noi too. The abbot said I could take him, but I must pay 5000 baht. I said I would not pay for an animal because I knew even then that this can actually feed the animal problem by creating a supply and demand chain, but I called Leonie and she said to pay him, which she would reimburse me, because it would give the animal a better life. So I thought that it must be standard, that paying to rescue an animal was normal. Now I know differently."

On the journey from Pa La-u to his home, a wild elephant crossed the road in front of Edwin's vehicle. Despite days spent in Kaeng Krachan National Park, it was the first time he had seen an elephant in the wild and until that moment, he had only seen wild elephant droppings, but never an elephant in the flesh.

"As a matter of fact, my friends and I used to joke that the tourism authorities would sneak out in the night and put elephant droppings on the road to make people think they were there," he says. "It was a constant joke between us."

He recalls the sight of that beast in front of his car like a snapshot in his mind.

Noi (which is Thai for little) settled in. Because of his growing knowledge of different species' needs, Edwin chained him to a coconut tree at night so he could climb up to sleep and he came down during the day. Noi had a hatred for women which meant interacting with the human Noi was off limits and would try to bite them, but other than that and occasionally escaping, he was a model gibbon houseguest.

A month passed and no one came to collect him, so Edwin built another large cage for Noi in his garden. It felt as if he was to have the monkeys permanently when Leonie told him the cage was ready for Friday and Kijke at Lopburi, but when he visited, there was no cage. He came home still their primary carer.

Leonie began to ask Edwin to do rescues on the weekends. On his first rescue, late in 1999, he was asked to collect two gibbons from a couple in Pattaya who had been keeping them as pets. Leonie wanted them taken to the facility in Bangkok. But the gibbons panicked when Edwin and a WAR representative tried to extract them from their large enclosure and load them into the truck; one went berserk attacking its owner. The insertion of 40 stitches was required to repair the damage. Edwin and his partner had to chase the gibbon into the house where they finally got sleeping pills into it and had to wait four hours for them to take effect.

"It was a fuck-up, a mess. We should have had a vet there with anaesthesia; we were completely unprepared," he says. "I seriously questioned my capability of being able to rescue any wildlife, but the people at WAR told me not to worry, that it happened sometimes even to the best. I know now that is not true, but it was a lie that gave me the confidence to continue."

He persisted, subsequently making successful collections of a macaque from a market and a gibbon from a roadside shop. Edwin says he always learnt best through doing and that sometimes meant making mistakes. And his familiar mode of learning continued in wildlife care, high intensity and at full pace. Inside, he felt cool and purposeful, a little wild and tough. He also felt part of a team, even having stickers made that said 'wild animal rescue' to put on his truck, but although he had a sense of purpose and enjoyed the rush of rescuing a creature from an enslaved life, he says now he had little real idea of what he was doing.

"I knew my place was not the right home for these monkeys and gibbons. I knew I was not the person who should ideally be saving them because I did not have a proper facility. But I knew I could treat them very well, and I knew I was the best they had at the time. I was not giving them up."

Kijke is still living with Friday at WFFT today, in an open field, now wild and free.

Edwin had begun to feel disenchanted with being a part of the fashion industry. With some exceptions, he found those who earned a living from trends and temporary desires for trinkets to be fake and flighty. He felt he did not fit into that and that those people followed fashion like a religion in the resulting uniformity of how they lived, what they ate and drank and what they drove. He still likens it to a cult where the pressure to conform was oppressive, and if you are not within, you are rejected and cast out.

He wanted to change to something else – he was not sure what – in business. He could see a change in mood where customers were beginning to ask for lower prices and his clients to pay later with long-range credit. Financial times were shifting in the 1990s in the wake of the excesses of the 1980s, and he realised his business had to be nimble to continue to meet the new needs. But Noi resisted his suggested changes in business practice and focus. She wanted the business to continue to serve the market in the current ways.

Things had become strained at home and because the couple worked together, at the business too. Niggles became fights. The silent treatment began to become a standard weapon in the breaks between battles. There were secrets and lies.

"I tried hard because I missed that feeling of the first flush of a relationship," Edwin says. "I wanted to feel in love again; the feeling of really mattering to someone else. In the whole of my life since, I was never to feel that again, if I am honest. I had it once, but it was never to be again for me. I definitely had relationships later that were an improvement, but that feeling of being crazy in love was a one-off."

The fighting got worse and acrimony increased. Because isolation is better than misery, Edwin and Noi began to live separate lives but struggled on for several more years under the same roof. Edwin was worried about their assets being intermingled and says he could not see a way of extracting himself without losing everything.

That fear was founded.

"We were talking through those last years, but no one was listening. It just became normal for us. In its way, it was sad, but that was just how it was," he says. "I think that we can come to accept even the worst of situations in order to cope."

Edwin says, as he now reflects on his relationship history, he sees it as a strangely haphazard component of an otherwise deliberately lived, disciplined life.

"To be honest, I never really know why I am with a girl, except for Marianne, whom I would have devoted my life to," he says. "I kind of walk into it. You sleep together, and then after sex, she stays over and then you are sharing five nights out of seven. And then you keep some things at each other's place and suddenly, she is there.

"If there was one thing I would have done differently in my life, it is in my relationships with women. I have never had a relationship where it has not gone that way – kind of sliding in without deliberately choosing it. They kind of come into my life and they stay."

Edwin admits that he had many years of not being happy in his personal relationship with Noi nor in his professional life with EFA, but he felt utterly trapped because he felt wound tightly into a framework of his own making. He put the part of himself that wanted stimulation and joy aside, accepting that this might be just how his life had worked out. He became used to being alone, to feeling isolated. He had made his own bed, and maybe this was what constituted lying in it, he reasoned.

"I think I could have accommodated anything," he says. "I was not really sure how it was going to work out, but it would somehow, some way. I think that perhaps I thought I would just die slowly inside.

"But then I woke up on the hood of my car."

5. I'm Still Standing

The splinter of glass and grinding crunch of folding metal in late October, 1999, were to be the crescendo that heralded a huge upheaval for Edwin. It was a sudden, violent event, but its consequences were to burn slowly.

Edwin had been on business in Chumpon, about three hours south of Cha-Am.

"It was a Friday night, and I had been there for my work with my personal assistant," he says. "We had been out to dinner, but I had not been drinking which was unusual at the time. I would normally drink with dinner, and I never worried about driving afterwards. We left about 7:30 pm in my grey Toyota SR5, and we were on the southern outskirts of Cha-Am when it happened. It was after midnight, and I fell asleep on the Hua Hin Bypass."

The car left the road and nosedived into a centre ravine between the two sides of the highway. The ditch had been made boggy by the sticky mud of the rainy season. It somehow missed trees in close proximity on either side, and when it came to rest, the front of the vehicle was a crumpled can that was hardly recognisable as a four-wheel drive. While his personal assistant was unhurt, Edwin was not wearing a seatbelt and the impact threw him through the broken windshield and deposited him, sprawled, onto the hood. He lay bruised and bleeding, with a head knock and a deep cut that resembled a semi-scalping. When Edwin came to and realised where he was, all he could think of was how to get away from the scene, a reaction he says now does not make complete sense but he considers was probably a result of survival instinct kicking in. In Thailand, law enforcement and emergency services do not automatically follow on from major car accidents; people are often expected to look after themselves.

"I got my computer from the back seat, left the car and hitchhiked with a truck driver to my home," he says. "The police came to my home the next morning and asked Noi what had happened and which hospital I was in. They presumed from the wreck that I was severely injured."

The officers and Noi found Edwin in his bedroom, by now the couple each had their own sleeping quarters, and found him lying in bed with blood spattering the sheets and floor from his head wound. Edwin woke with a start, and quickly realised it was painful to breathe because his ribs were broken and his lungs bruised.

"The first thing you feel is that you are glad to be alive; I think that is natural," he says. "I recall feeling that I was so invincible that even this terrible accident could not fucking kill me. I was a winner and felt high about it. I know now that might have been a standard initial reaction.

"But if you are smart enough, you soon also see that you could have died that day. You realise you have been given another chance that maybe you did not deserve, and you have to change the things in your life that are not working to make the best of that. I eventually understood that, but it took a couple of pushes and pokes between the eyes to make me follow through."

Within a week of the crash, Edwin went to his accountant to ask if he had enough cash flow to get a new car or whether the wrecked one, despite being in a sorry state, must be repaired.

"He said to me: 'My god, Edwin. Do you care about the car you drive and the business you have more than you care about your life? You could have been killed.'

"That was the moment. That was it. That changed everything for me because it brought it home.

"In the 1980s, Prince had this song *1999,* and when it came out, I always thought I would not make it. I had this feeling I would not make it to 1999; I now know I was lucky to see the year 2000."

Edwin began discussions with Noi that had been years in the making, that should have occurred when the gulf between them began to be a bigger part of their relationship than their togetherness. The exchanges were painful, he says, but he felt a calm about the inevitability of the separation and relief that there would no longer be the insufferable tension caused by neither of them being happy with the other. Noi moved out, leaving Edwin in their beautiful house.

They continued to work together, thinking that they were professional enough to manage dealing with each other every day as they began the messy business of unbinding their entwined lives. A short period of insecurity for Edwin followed when it was not clear to him where he should go: continue to follow the money in a new business venture or to follow his heart into something bigger. He says he was not looking for a new lover, but a new love: pursuit of a purpose and a passion.

The fallout of the separation was in some ways more traumatic that the split itself. Most of their mutual friends chose to side with her.

"It is extraordinary to me that when a relationship ends, people chose a victim and feel sympathy for them, when really, sometimes things just die," he says. "Relationships end, and there is rarely just one person to blame. Everyone is a victim, but outsiders looking in treat it like a game, a scandal."

The last straw for Edwin was a New Year's Eve party he threw for his staff to herald in the new millennium. It was a lavish affair with live music, a stage, lights and disco balls, wait staff and beautiful catered food. Loving a party and knowing this one was to mark a significant moment in time and probably in his life, Edwin spared no expense.

"At the end of the party, I did not hear one word of thanks. It was devastating," Edwin says. "The staff were complaining that they either had no bonus, or for those who got one, it was not big enough. After that, I said to myself 'maybe I need to start thinking about what I need, what I want'. I thought about what my Jewish boss in Antwerp – who had survived for years in the Auschwitz camp in World War II – told me when I was 20 and was being a particular pain the ass to him at work; he would say to me, 'Edwin, I wish you a lot of staff'."

Edwin had had enough of continuing in a line of work he no longer loved just to keep others employed. As well as feeling personally unappreciated and disrespected, the business was not doing as well as before. One of his larger customers in the UK had not paid their bill, and others were similarly slowing in their orders and payments. Edwin had interest from a few other businesses to buy his set-up, and he even offered to continue to work for a time in sales to ease the transition to new ownership, but each proposal fell through.

At this time, Noi and a manager started to move machinery out of the facility and shift money from accounts, and Noi started to take things from the house when Edwin was at work. Then Edwin found his personal bank account was blocked because Noi had started legal action for a property and assets settlement. He says he had brought shame on her family by their relationship breaking down, and the family wanted him to suffer because of that as well. The situation spiralled up, the rancour accelerating.

Then Noi complained to the police that Edwin had hit her, something he says he would never do because hitting a woman in anger disgusts him. He attended the police station for an interview, during which time his motorbike and TV were taken from the house. He was released without charge due to the absence of evidence, but the accusation had dragged the fallout from the split to a whole new low among friends and family.

But worse was to come. Edwin was formally told by local police that a contract had been taken out on his life. In March 2000, they issued him with a police sergeant bodyguard known as Johnny Two Guns. He was a 'black hand', one who was brought in to finish troublesome business. He moved in with Edwin, securing the house and carrying an automatic weapon when they ventured out. While it all seemed surreal and in some ways exciting to be part of a real-life crime drama, after a couple of months, Edwin had had enough. He left his Cha-Am beachfront home in the dead of night so that no one knew where he was going.

Edwin says that at the start of his working life, he thought his business acumen would leave a lasting memento to the world, that he would eventually be remembered as the founder of a business that made goods that decorated people's bodies and lives. But that now felt empty, temporary and frivolous, and he needed to leave it all behind.

"I knew I wanted to do this. I knew I wanted to do something more meaningful, better, bigger than just make fashion accessories and garments and ship them out," he says. "What I wanted to do had to be sustainable; it had to do good for the wider world. And it had to do something for those who might not be able to do it for themselves.

"It sounds simple, and in a way it is. But I am also aware that *I* wanted to do it – me. It may sound selfish – it is, I suppose – but it was my dream, and I wanted to feel good about it too.

"And it had to be for the animals."

6. Just like Starting Over

Four months after Edwin and Noi separated, Edwin had taken up with another Thai beauty, Chanapa Manuchan, or Pha as she was known; and with her and his animals, late that night, Edwin drove to Wild Animal Rescue Foundation in Bangkok to develop a plan for developing a rescue centre together.

"I knew it was the end of an era. I knew my life, as it had been, was over," Edwin says. "I'll admit that I cried that first night out of fear and grief for what I left behind. I knew I could not stay in Cha-Am, and I could not go back to Holland because I did not have access to money to settle back there at that time. I was scared for perhaps the first time ever. But I pulled myself together in the night. When I stopped crying like a little boy, I began to plan. I soon worked out which letters I needed to write and what action I needed to take to access the money that had been frozen by Noi.

"And I was with a pretty, fun girl who was in her early 20s, and by this time, I was 34. By the morning, I felt hope, and I could look forward. At the time, I was stressed, but I knew something else, hopefully something better, was ahead."

Edwin's vision began to take shape in his busy mind. The rescue centre he conjured was to be a multi-species facility; the first of its kind in the country to take all manner of creatures and to turn none away. In his mind's eye, it would complement the gibbon rescue centre WAR ran in Phuket. But while his ideas had taken hold, they could not yet take form: for six months, Edwin was holed up, effectively hiding in Bangkok. He had lost it all, biding his time until the strings of his broken relationship were finally cut so he could truly start afresh. The problem was that he had no cash flow. He was on the breadline, living hand to mouth. Edwin borrowed money from family, and he got a job with a cable TV company for a few months to pay the bills.

"The owner of this company, a German ex-pat, opened my eyes about how others did business in Thailand," he says. "This man treated his staff and even his own daughter as personal slaves. He shouted and belittled people, and when I challenged him on it, he hid behind the 'I've got diabetes' excuse. It was a time of survival for me. I needed the job, so it was hard to cope with a person like that. And after six months, I had had more than enough and was happy to leave. My then-boss died in a car accident two years later."

While the focus on a wildlife rescue centre burned bright, treading water in time was difficult for a man as results-driven, impatient and in need of action as Edwin. To use the time more fruitfully, Edwin visited WAR's centre in Phuket, asking questions about how funds were arranged and observing how that facility worked, how the animals were cared for and how the operation was kept afloat with the help of well-intentioned, animal-welfare focused paying volunteers. He noted that almost all the money from the volunteer contributions and tourist visits was sent to Bangkok to keep the office 'running'.

Edwin felt determined to run his future centre differently, with the focus on the rescued animals front and centre. But he also found he had few supporters, with even some family members pointing out that he was not a biologist, veterinarian or zoologist and had little idea of what he was doing. While he accepted that they were technically right, still the notion that he must change the way of things for the animals would not leave him. He had spent a lot of time learning as much as he could about the needs of the various animal species and about their natural behaviours and diets.

Edwin has an extraordinary capacity to learn; his complete fluency in five languages is testament to that, and he applied this to animals. He bought books about anaesthesia, husbandry and primates and devoured them. He memorised the then-264 known primate species of the world, what they looked like and what their characteristics were. He bought books on wildlife and primates in Thailand, read them thoroughly and then marked the sub-species off as they crossed his path. He then did the same with birds.

"I don't have a photographic memory, but if I could liken it to a computer, I don't have a good storage system in my mind, but I have a very big RAM. I find it easy to retain a lot of information quickly if I am interested in a topic," he says. "It is funny now to think now that when I first saw a langur, I thought it was a long-tail macaque. And the first gibbon I ever saw was in a bar in Bangkok, dressed up in a beer garden in Sukhumvit Road in Bangkok."

He had learnt to handle the animals and dart them if necessary to move them, so he felt he was not a complete novice, despite the naysayers.

"It is like when I buy an appliance. I just get it out of the box, and I use it: I am not the kind of person who reads the manual. If it is broken, I try to fix it myself. I learn mostly by doing, after some initial assessment."

For Edwin, the early days of his new wildlife-focused life were tough, but it was also freeing in its way.

"I lived on noodle soup, fried rice and a couple of beers every day for a long time. But I didn't worry about anything, honestly, because I had just escaped death in an accident. I might have lost everything, but I realised I had been living in the clouds, and until that accident, I did not realise how much of an asshole I was. I did not realise I was wasting time on things that were absolutely unimportant.

"That was at the front of my mind at all times for a long time afterwards."

Edwin knew unequivocally that he needed to rescue the animals that should have been as wild as those he had seen free and full of life in Kaeng Krachan National Park but were kept in captivity. He was fired up by the injustice of it, the unfairness, and while he knew he had little knowledge about how to do it properly, he knew he could provide better life for those that might come into his care. He knew that rescued animals could not be immediately released into the wild and that time and care needed to be taken to help them rediscover their wild instincts. He wanted to provide a safe, healthy place to help them endure that reconversion.

For decades, it has been legal to own elephants in Thailand; they are regarded as property. And while Thailand's native animals were protected by the government and government officials could seize them from people at any time, they rarely did because they had no way of accommodating them and little knowledge about how to properly keep them. Thus, baby monkeys, gibbons, slow loris and otters were taken from the wild to become people's playthings, merchandise and pets. The animals also proved to be lucrative photo props to make more than a few dollars from the passing tourist trade.

Edwin says that while WAR's intention was sound, even to his inexperienced eye, the lack of infrastructure and space for animals were concerning, and he felt strongly that the animals needed something better. He and Leonie had a strong professional relationship and much of his initial knowledge of gibbons came from her.

There were no guidelines on rescue when Edwin's fledgling moves into the field began. There were effectively no animal welfare regulations in Thailand, no rules on how animals should be kept. But there were rules on what was legal to keep and rescuing illegally-kept creatures drove his passion.

He felt he could not wait any longer. Through July and August in 2000, he used 600,000 baht of the funds he had gained access to in Europe to begin building a wildlife rescue centre for WAR in Khao Kra Puk in Phetchaburi province. The abbot at a local Buddhist temple said Edwin could use a piece of land to house his animals and charged 20,000 baht a month rent for it. It was on the edge of a national park, a beautiful, thickly forested area rich in flora and fauna.

The support he found was mixed: some friends, including prominent hotel manager Robert Rijnders, looked after Edwin in those lean years; one Dutch friend helped him set up what was the first incarnation of WFFT but charged interest on payments for his time. Some of Edwin's old business colleagues offered some funds for cage construction.

Edwin's girlfriend Pha had a brother, Pranom Manuchan – Nom – who had been working as a foot masseur and said he wanted to help Edwin with the animals. He was good with his hands and had some construction knowledge and was not scared of hard work. Edwin jumped at the extra labour, and the pair worked well together. Edwin says life had a simplicity he had not experienced before, and he loved that. He rented an old farmhouse for a tiny price. He had a new dream, and now the whiff of a new life to build it on.

"We built some beautiful cages and spaces for monkeys, with vines for them to climb on and swing from. It was exactly what I wanted; it was exactly how I pictured it," he says. "I was very happy. It was as if my dream could be real and I could see that for the first time."

Edwin did have to adjust his sails a little as the wind was a bit stronger than he had anticipated; he had expected to take in mainly primates, maybe some slow lorises, but not much other wildlife. He thought growing his facility to accommodate maybe 30 or 40 animals in total would be sufficient.

"I thought I would just take in animals, rehabilitate, get them back into the wild and then rescue new ones again," Edwin says. "That, of course, got completely out of hand. At that time, I had no clue that less than 30 per cent could ever go back to the wild. And I also did not factor in the life expectancy of some species. Gibbons, for example, can live for 45 years, so basically you just add and add to the numbers all the time."

Then came his first rescue. Edwin got a phone call from someone, who knew about his accidental acquisition of monkeys, telling him of Pepsi, who was kept in a little birdcage at a Cha-Am restaurant on the beach. The sight of the creature held in that way was distressing to the caller, and Edwin promised to look into his predicament. Now fluent in the Thai language and ways, Edwin convinced the owner to hand his over what was to him a simple curiosity for customers. Edwin picked up Pepsi and brought him home. The cheeky monkey found safety and space as he had not known it for his whole life, and Edwin was out of the blocks as an independent wildlife rescuer.

But then came a roadblock. An anonymous complaint was made about the calls of the animals and noise of the operation. An official from the then-Forestry department came to see Edwin, telling him the land was protected forestry area and had not been the abbot's to lease to him in the first place. The officials confirmed whispers from locals that the abbot was not a good character and was more interested in his own benefits than the needs of the community or the animals. He enjoyed many of the trappings that Buddhist monks are meant to eschew, such as having a fridge in his house and a gun under his bed. In the years to follow, he was eventually ousted from the temple – something Edwin thinks of now as karma catching up with him.

Once Edwin discovered the land and rent agreement was unlawful and unofficial, he refused to pay the abbot any more money. The rancour began. Threats were made against Edwin, Pha and Nom and, worse for him, the animals. Edwin began to worry the animals – which by now numbered about 30 – to whom he had promised safety and care were at real risk.

Edwin found himself at a fork in the road and knew he could not choose the easy option of shutting down and finding a quiet, regular life. Desperate, Edwin made a deal with the government to take most of his animals into their sub-standard facility until he could work out his next move. It was not ideal but at least they would be safe and would be fed until he developed a plan about what to do next. He planned to retain Kijke, Friday and Pepsi.

The situation between Edwin and those at WAR had also worsened, with suspicion on both sides and distrust taking root. Edwin says he reached a point of no return when financial reimbursements Leonie had promised did not appear, and he began to feel desperately deflated.

Late in 2000 a New Zealand team from National Geographic came and filmed a segment at Edwin's rescue facility as part of prize he had been awarded for his animal rescue work. A central part of the Heroes for the Planet prize was a car from Ford, and despite waiting and being told it was on the way, it never arrived. He made inquiries and found that the holdup was not with Ford, but with Leonie. The vehicle had not been delivered to him because Leonie kept it in Bangkok. But there was more: included in the award was $US50,000 to set up a clinic and despite promises, this was also not transferred. In a moment of clarity, Edwin realised he was part of a system that was putting animal care second to financial gain, and he felt the urgent need to extract himself from it.

"When the money did not come and the vehicle did not come, and I found out why, I was certainly worried, but I was new to this. I really needed the car, and I really needed the money to start up a little clinic to help with animal care, but I thought this must be normal or that there was some sort of other system I would benefit from later," Edwin says. "But then I met with some people from Wildlife Conservation Society in Kaeng Krachan National Park, where they were doing some research. And I met Tim Redford from Wild Aids, which became Freeland

Foundation, an organisation concerned with animal trafficking. They gave me some information about WAR that really concerned me, but I felt that maybe they were jealous or something. After a while, the stories were consistent and constant. I felt I had been screwed both ways; by the monk and by WAR. But that sort of thing just makes me fight harder; I was not ready to give it all up." By January 2001, Edwin had decided to separate from WAR and go it alone with a centre but knew it had to be located somewhere else, and had not yet worked out a business strategy to make that happen.

Earlier, Leonie had told Edwin that she was increasingly concerned with the amount of time he was spending travelling back and forth from his home to Hua Hin 45km away and said she might be able to arrange access to the internet through the telephone line in the phone box outside his home. She said they could then more easily do the business communications via email, which at the time involved dial-up access. So she sent someone from Bangkok to tap the line so that at night, he could dial up to send and receive emails and get business done online.

"I never actually used it, but the connection was there, and it was linked to my house, so I was responsible," he says. "She then called me on a Saturday in February, saying tomorrow she would be coming to discuss the future of my rescue centre and that there had been some funding come in to secure it. It sounded odd to me. It felt fishy.

"Then it hit me like an icy shower; I had overstayed on my visa by two months because my passport was with a lawyer at WAR's request, because they said they were arranging my work permit which never happened. I felt I was being set up."

Edwin contacted the lawyer and said he needed to pick up his passport to make copies. He collected the passport on the Sunday morning and went to Ranong in southern Thailand where he had professional contacts and had positive dealings with officials during his years in business. With their help and advice, he paid the 20,000 baht overstay fine so he could remain in the country.

On the Monday morning, a police contingent including a colonel from Bangkok raided Edwin's home, wanting to arrest him for his visa overstay and also for a federal offence of grand theft for stealing the telephone line – infrastructure technically owned by the government. Because he was in Ranong at the time, an arrest warrant was issued, and he was to be arrested. He returned home two days later. The police were surprised that he had cleared the visa overstay matter, and that charge was dropped, but the more serious theft charge stood. Edwin was fingerprinted and a mugshot was taken.

"In one way, in your head you know you did not know you did anything wrong, but you also hear about foreigners rotting in Thai prisons for nothing at all, and I worried that I could be the next one. I could actually see that in my mind, and it made me feel sick," Edwin says. "While I felt I had some support from one or two of the local police, it felt like a kind of twilight zone, and it could go one way or the other."

The village chief, whom Edwin had befriended and who admired his work with the animals, signed Edwin's bail undertaking, and he was released until the courts could determine his fate. But Edwin's biggest fear was that they would take Kijke, Friday and Pepsi. It became evident he was being watched by law enforcement officers, and he felt he must get his trio to a safe haven.

Edwin had rescued a leopard, Som Chai, who was blind in one eye and missing most of his tail but would make loud noises when Edwin played with him. To the untrained ear, it sounded ferocious, so play with him, Edwin did. The officers on watch that night heard the big cat growling and came to investigate. This offered a chance to escape from the back of the property, and Nom and two boys from the village took the monkeys in a cage and drove them to a safe house in Hua Hin. The officers were none the wiser.

As soon as it was dark, Edwin picked up the animals from Hua Hin and drove them to Highland Farm, a gibbon rescue centre he trusted in Mae Sot, in western Thailand near the border with Burma – a nine-hour drive away. He swore the owners to secrecy, and they agreed to keep the monkeys for as long as it took for Edwin to get a new centre up and running. The trio stayed there for about eight months before Edwin could take them back.

Then Edwin officially severed ties with WAR. They insisted on coming to observe the removal of the more than 30 animals from the initial facility. They noted that Friday, Kijke and Pepsi were missing and asked that Edwin be charged with theft of their property. The forestry department official, to whom Edwin had explained his affection for the trio, claimed the WAR count of animals had been incorrect and that all animals had been taken under their authority and into their centre.

"I needed to know those three were effectively still in my care, even though they were by now far away," Edwin says. "I needed them to stay focused on what I would do next, knowing they needed me to start over because I could give them and others like them good lives. They symbolised the future for me." It took two and a half years of fighting, and Edwin was eventually cleared of the theft of government property charge.

The animals given over to the government from the initial centre were never returned. Som Chai, the one-eyed, tail-less leopard, died in 2017 after years of being used in a government breeding program.

With Nom and Pha, Edwin had gone to the head monk at Khao Luk Chang, about 15km from Khao Krapuk, who was the most senior abbot in the district, to apologise for his unknowing involvement with the unscrupulous monk and the disruption it had caused in one of his villages. On a subsequent visit to him on the day the rescued animals had been taken into the government's care, the abbot was sitting with the mayor of Khao Luk Chang, who had sourced and sold Edwin many of the construction materials for the first centre.

"The mayor said to me, 'If you can't have the rescue centre in Khao Krapuk, we would like to have it in Khao Luk Chang. A lot of people bring monkeys and gibbons to the temples in the area, and they don't know how to look after them. A centre like yours might bring foreigners in and you might be able to teach English to the monks and the children in school.' But I said I did not have much money because Noi was still blocking my accounts. I said I could borrow about a million baht from business contacts, but I needed more."

The abbot said he would provide temple land for a facility and would supply electricity and allow the pumping of water from the lake, which Edwin could filter and use. He said there was ground water that could be accessed via a well after the centre was up and running.

"There were a few positive thoughts in my head at this offer. I could see what was ahead, and it looked good, but I had a few doubting thoughts about whether I had the energy to start it all again," Edwin says. "But then I was thrown a lifeline. My Finnish friend Tom Frisk, who had helped me so very much in my other life, said he would come to help me and gave me enough money – just gave it, unlike so many others – to build a little four-room house to be able to take in four volunteers. I felt supported and that gave me enough energy to start. You do not forget those kindnesses, and I will always think of Tom as one of the co-founders of the foundation." Tom died in 2017, and regularly visited the rescue centre with his wife until close to the end of his life.

Construction of the simple concrete structure was quick: two rooms were set aside for four volunteers to sleep in, Edwin and Pha moved into the third room and Nom lived in the fourth. A basic open-air space with a small kitchen and place for seating and meetings adjoined the rooms. The structure remains and is the volunteer house today.

Edwin put half a million baht in to start up the project, money he initially had to borrow from a colleague, and began to build his wildlife rescue dream afresh. Saliently, he and Tom – after a couple of drinks together – came up with the name Wildlife *Friends* Foundation Thailand, as a contrast to WAR.

"The only time I can remember sleeping well in my life was in that window of time, when I was starting up WFFT," Edwin says. "I had nothing to lose then and everything to gain. Now, even when things are going well, I worry about when it is going to stop.

"Those early months of WFFT were the most peaceful, and while physically it was hard work, it was in many ways most mentally relaxed time of my life."

7. Ain't Necessarily So

False starts and stumbles often knock out the best of competitors, even those with great commitment and intention. Others use disappointment as fuel for the fire and go harder and stronger, and this was always going to be the way for Edwin.

He had effectively road-tested a rescue centre at Khao Krapuk and made errors of judgement in trusting the wrong people there. And while his gut told him that the new location was a good fit and that the temple land on the lake's edge at Khao Luk Chang had all the feel of solid ground for his operation, he wanted to get the structure of the set-up absolutely right.

Edwin has always been a man who operates out of his head, constantly assessing and weighing up information. When he is in the zone, he has a steel-trap mind that can compute information at lightning speed, and he uses logic in a way that often verges on clinical. In almost all regards, he is unabashedly tough. But to see him in the presence of a wild animal in need of care, something else emerges from within him. He is effusive and loving, kind and respectful. When these exchanges are underway, it is clear that inside Edwin, deep compassion can rest beside an utter lack of sentimentality: strange bedfellows indeed.

Edwin was not going to mess up the second chance of giving form to his dreams of giving rescued wildlife the safety and security they were so sorely lacking. And this time he wanted to get it absolutely right. Edwin knew he did not want to set the facility up as a business which would in effect be about making money from the animals' misfortune. He wanted a foundation that would be sustainable, an entity that could grow and would not be dependent on him alone for its survival.

Again, though, he was to be taught some hard lessons, this time by a Dutch ex-pat businessman who knew of his financial predicament and whom Edwin thought was a friend offering to become a partner and set it up as a business investment. The Heroes for the Planet episode was being aired in Europe and people were aware of Edwin's work, so he saw it as a way of gaining leverage from the PR. He told Edwin he thought there was a lot of money to be made, and he wanted to invest in the project.

He gave Edwin 300,000 baht in cash and paid a discounted price for his lawyer to set up the Foundation. But the board was listed as Edwin's friend, the friend's personal assistant and the lawyer. The lawyer then began to agitate to have Edwin removed from the project, spreading rumours that he was of poor character and was more a shrewd businessman than a wildlife warrior. But the abbot of the Khao Luk Chang temple stepped in, supporting Edwin, saying his agreement for the use of the land on which the centre rested was with Edwin, not with the Foundation.

Ultimately, Edwin paid the friend his money back with interest, dissolved the first incarnation of the Foundation and restructured it so that on the board was him, the village chief and the abbot. He then cut all ties with the so-called friend.

He could not be happier with that structure, which has remained in place ever since.

"People seem to think that I like confrontation, but I don't actually," he says. "I find it exhausting and time wasting, but I am capable of just wiping a person from my life, and that is what I did with this Dutchman. You have to just shut the door and move on sometimes."

While Edwin knew what he needed to begin the functional work of WFFT, Edwin also knew he needed loads of help to create something so large. A small Hua Hin magazine article announced to the community that a centre purpose-built to take in rescued wildlife was in its embryonic stage and needed material support in the form of metal, screws and wire to build cages and enclosures. Edwin was touched by the donations of materials and offers of manual help from the community.

They were quickly ready to take in animals.

A few weeks later, a Channel 7 breakfast show broadcast out of Bangkok picked up on the article, and invited Edwin on to talk about his vision for the captive wildlife of Thailand. Edwin took along images of the first rescue centre, visually demonstrating the need for rescued animals to be given safe haven and secure environments in which to begin a freer, more natural life. The appeal of doing good for animals, sold through Edwin's personal charisma and easy way of communicating his concerns for animals, made for engaging viewing. This was the first national broadcast about the project, and the response was overwhelming.

"By the time I got out of the studio, I had so many missed calls on my phone from people who wanted to give up their animals because they had showed my number on the screen during the interview. I was quite stunned, and a little overwhelmed about the obvious need out there," he says.

"A woman who called had a white-cheeked gibbon and a black agile gibbon she wanted to give up, and as I had never seen a white-cheeked gibbon, I knew these needed to be the first of our rescues."

With Nom, Edwin quickly constructed two abutting enclosures in preparation for these premiere arrivals and made arrangements to pick them up from a home in Rat Buri, west of Bangkok. On arrival that Saturday morning, the animals were darted, and he loaded them into his car and set out on the two-hour journey to the new centre.

On the way back, about 10 km before the Petchaburi province capital, the wildlife warriors struck a traffic jam. Ever hungry for information, and aware that the apes aboard were on the clock before their anaesthetic wore off, Edwin tuned into the police channel on the radio he had aboard his four-wheel drive Toyota to find out the cause for the delay.

It became apparent that minutes earlier, a car had hit a bridge ahead and had torpedoed its five occupants into the river. Initial police information was that a baby was among the victims. Never one to be a passive observer, Edwin told Nom he was going in. They skirted the traffic by driving beside the road, arriving at the bridge within a minute or two. In his hurry, Edwin parked the vehicle at a rakish angle on the roadside, leaving Nom to watch the car and monitor the sleeping gibbons.

With heart racing and adrenalin pumping, Edwin approached the rescue team and one of the witnesses to ask where the people had entered the water. He calculated that the child was likely to have floated downstream in the moving water, being lighter and more buoyant.

Into the water he went, and in the fervour of the moment, forgot to take off his shoes and take his mobile phone from his pocket. He was seeking the heaviest of the adult occupants, figuring they would still be near the point of entry.

"I could not see anything; the water was churned up. I was diving in and feeling for a person, a limb, a head, anything. I first found an arm, but it was someone else who was also diving. And suddenly I left a lifeless arm, a tiny forearm. It had to be a child and that surprised me, because I thought a small person would have floated downstream. I pulled it up, straight up and struggled a little, but found the surface and swam to the side with this kid. I was wired, operating on instinct, and I guess just using my water rescue knowledge. I started CPR on the little girl, but the rescue team and the paramedics who had arrived quickly took over the resuscitation. I dived back in to try to find more."

Within minutes, Edwin had fished three people out of the river. But he continued to dive and search, thinking about where the people might be, feeling with his hands and particularly desperate to find the baby. After 20 minutes, Edwin was exhausted and realised that the chance of finding survivors was lost. He dragged himself out of the water and lay spread-eagled on the bridge on his back, eyes closed as he tried to catch his breath. The gravity of what had occurred and the awfulness of being so close to the lives traumatically snatched momentarily made him still.

At that moment, a van with people from Khao Luk Chang was returning from Bangkok, where the villagers had attended a meeting. With horror, as they were waved through, they saw Edwin lying on the bridge, drenched and still. They noted that his four-wheel drive was on the bridge shoulder, lodged at a strange angle. They saw Nom, stressed and pacing and immediately called back to the village, reporting that Edwin had been in an accident and was dead on the bridge.

A posse from the village came to give Pha and Tom Frisk, who was visiting, the terrible news of Edwin's passing. Pha tried to reach him on his phone, which was waterlogged and unresponsive. To everyone, Edwin was dead. The dream was over before it had truly begun.

Two hours later, Edwin and Nom drove into the centre with the now wide-awake gibbons, damp and dirty. For the grieving people assembled, the shock of a death was rapidly exchanged for the jolt of survival. To the villagers and the staff at the centre, it was as if Edwin had died and been reborn: a kind of earthy, primal, animal-accompanied resurrection.

Of the five who had been flung into the water that day, only the six-year-old – a niece of the driver – was to survive. The baby's lifeless body was found days later between the river mouth and the sea.

A reunion with the surviving little girl a short while later was accompanied by a thank you gift of flowers and banana fritters. Edwin can still recall the scent of the food and the deep emotion of that day.

"When there is trouble, I am in there. I can't just sit on my hands. It is not about doing good or being the hero, but about the primitive need to preserve a life. I don't consciously think about it, but I do know that it is a need as much as other people might have a need to not be involved.

"I do not walk away from trouble, ever. But I have been accused several times of looking for it, too."

WFFT was soon up and running. Processes were bedded down and the initial construction phase came to a close, enabling the little team to respond to rescue requests and accommodate incoming animals.

And Edwin had love in his life: he had Pha to share his new purpose and passion, and they were happy for a time. They shared a birthday, she was visually beautiful and would play guitar and sing in the evenings. Edwin has always loved music, and this tugged at his heartstrings.

"I was proud to be with her: she was pretty and fun and cute. I had taken her away from a life in a bar where she had been more than just a barmaid and given her a better life. She looked at me with eyes that were soft and loving, and I liked that feeling. I liked to feel loved by such a beautiful, fun girl.

"She was a bit of a rescue; I see that now I look back. That might sound a bit rude, but in many ways it was true because I had helped give her something better than she had. She changed and was hard working and made beautiful food. She brought me happiness."

He had some challenges as well. In 2002, over a period of time a couple of the white-handed gibbons he had rescued got sick and then died after a few days, and he could not work out why.

"I thought to myself, *Here I am without a biology or veterinary degree, and I am trying to take care of animals, and they are dying.* By the time the third one died, I thought maybe I am not the right person to do this."

But Edwin felt a responsibility to help the ones still living, so he took the last one that had died – a black baby called Mango – to the National Institute of Animal Health in Bangkok where a professor took a great interest in the case. She asked for the bodies of those that had died and found it was a parasite called strongyloides. It was solved simply, she wrote a paper on it, and Edwin was able to share what he had learnt with other people who had gibbons and monkeys to keep them safe.

"It was about animal management, animal health. I was learning every day about new ways to help them, and it made me feel that those animals did not die for nothing."

The concern and care with which Edwin deals with animals is remarkable. He honours them entirely, appreciating their many facets and seeing them as whole beings that have many needs, just like humans. To watch him interact with a rescued animal is to understand the depth of their importance to him. He positions himself with them as one in authority but also one they can trust.

But Edwin says he has learnt to hold a little part of himself back, the part that if given would break his heart when they die. That part has already been jettisoned, handed over without him realising it to a big, beautiful boy named Meow.

Meow was a tiger Edwin rescued from a petrol station just outside of Cha-Am in May, 2001. He took a call from Uncle Teng, the owner of the service station, who said he had a tiger he wanted to be rid of because a local vet had said it was about to die. Meow, who was fully grown, had a chest infection, but that was secondary to an infection he had acquired in a dirty spaying by the vet who had never sterilised a tiger before. Meow had been de-clawed in his infancy to make him 'safe' and poor nutrition had left him with permanent spinal damage. He had also been chained up for a long time as a kind of tourist attraction, with concrete and gravel at his feet and the fumes of the petrol and passing traffic as company.

"Basically he was dying, and Uncle Teng, a man I liked, did not want him to die there. He would rather he died under my care," Edwin says. "That was the only reason he wanted to give me the tiger."

Edwin was still in touch with Johnny Two Guns, and Johnny came with him to pick up the tiger and ensure the correct paperwork was lodged for it at the police station at the nearby.

"When you pull up at a police station with a tiger in the back of a truck, everyone comes out," Edwin says. "The police chief says, 'this is a tiger, a protected species. You can't have it.' I had the paperwork for it, but Johnny spoke up and said not to worry, that everything was in order. 'Who the fuck are you?' the police chief asked him. 'I'm Johnny', Johnny Two Guns says. Another of the police officers said he knew him from Cha-Am. 'Don't mess with him; you had better be careful. He is well connected'."

That is how Meow came to live at WFFT. For the first weeks, he could not sit up and could not walk, so he lived on the floor in Edwin's bedroom. Edwin hand-fed him small pieces of meat, chopped bone and small pieces of offal.

"About three weeks later, I was awoken by this tiger licking my face. He could not have done that before because he could not sit up, and I felt very happy because I knew it meant he was getting better," Edwin says. "A week more passed, and he had to get out of my room because he was trying to get on the bed. Pha was not too pleased about it because he was a big tiger."

In the first months of the new rescue centre, when Edwin wondered whether he had made the right decision in taking on the authorities and the system in setting up his centre, Meow became an affirming comfort. He was the confirmation that the decision was right and good and that the animals needed the kind of help his centre could offer.

An intensive period of physiotherapy and hydrotherapy followed, and by the end of the year, Meow was in relatively good health. He was playful, particularly with Edwin and would lick his face, arms and legs, much as a cat would. Edwin spent a great deal of time with him, and they developed a strong bond. Meow's strange gait, which made him look as if he was walking carefully on a slippery surface, also made him a YouTube celebrity.

Edwin has taken on a black street dog named Sylvia the year before Meow came into his life, and the unlikely pair also developed a strong bond of play and companionship.

Meow's spinal issues, particularly compromising because of the way tigers' muscles and skeletons are structured, got suddenly worse in about 2012. When he could not walk any more, Meow was laid on hay in Edwin's carport so he could be easily turned. Edwin would sometimes curl up next to him for the night.

He died in 2013 while Edwin was in the CITES conference in Bangkok. Edwin broke down at the conference when he was told and says he felt a hollow, deep upset for months. In the quiet moments, Edwin still feels the aching hole that Meow's death left behind in his life.

"You get too involved, too close, and there is too much pain when they go," Edwin says. "Of course I get attached to some of the rescued animals, but I don't think I could ever become so deeply devoted as I was to Meow.

"He was my boy. He still is, in a way."

Today, every time Edwin opens his laptop, his background picture reminds him of that special kind of love; the photo shows him and his boy, face to face, playing in the water.

Under Thai law, animals kept at the centre need a permit because protected animals required registration. Edwin quickly learnt the system had loopholes and needed interpretation, sometimes with incongruous results. Much depended on the whims of the officials. Technically, WFFT is not allowed to rescue wildlife. And in rescuing animals and developing a business model to make the process sustainable, Edwin has rubbed some people up the wrong way.

In July 2001, Edwin was suddenly arrested again.

An American man with two daughters had claimed that Edwin had charged them a king's ransom for a day trip to the centre and then prevented them from leaving by refusing to take them to their hotel unless they paid him more. The trouble was, there were no organised day trips at that time.

In the course of that investigation, police arrested and charged Edwin with harassment and illegal wildlife possession. His case was reported in the news media.

A journalist from ITV, which became Thai PBS (with whom Edwin still has a good relationship) investigated, to discover that the hotel that the report claimed the Americans were staying at said they had no American guests with two children on those dates. The police investigated and interviewed the workers on site, and no one had seen any Americans. The entire episode was created from nothing, meant to intimidate and obstruct Edwin's operation. Edwin suspects the report emanated from someone within the non-government animal welfare sector.

The officials noted that the animals at the burgeoning centre – among them civets, monkeys, gibbons and Meow – were well cared for. Compared to the many animals kept at temples, the animals on this temple land were thriving. The provincial prosecutor was to be moved from Petchaburi to Rat Buri and had to clear his paperwork. The day he left, he officially dropped all charges against Edwin.

"The first couple of years were rough, certainly," Edwin says. "It made me very upset to realise that illegal wildlife traffickers, and I knew a few already by then, were not the major threat to me. It was sickening to realise at that time that other NGOs were my biggest problem, that the people who should be fighting with me for the same cause were fighting against me. I called one of them LAM – little angry man. That made me sick to the stomach, and the lack of trust I felt was very isolating."

But he had allies too, including Tim Redford from Freeland, who were genuinely concerned about illegal wildlife trafficking, and the poor welfare of kept wild animals and supported Edwin's work.

"Tim himself has been victim to extreme harassment by the same NGOs I had trouble with," Edwin says. "Only a few years before WFFT started, Tim was improving animal welfare in government facilities, but when a Thai child lost his arm at one of those places, Tim was blamed when he had no responsibility in the matter. He, like me, continued despite the difficulties, but unfortunately not in a hands-on way with the animals anymore."

But at last, Edwin felt he was giving rescued animals a life that was improved and safe. His vision had taken form. His confidence and knowledge had grown, at some cost.

"The truth is plain to me now that since 2001, I have been setting up and running a wildlife rescue centre against all rules, regulations and odds. But it was the right thing to do. When I look back, I don't know where I got the strength to keep going in those early years. I really don't understand it."

Support within the sector needs to be two-way for a strong community to be built. Edwin found this out when he was called on to look after animals in the wake of unthinkable horror.

Highland Farm, where Edwin had taken his monkeys to protect them from seizure in 2000, had been founded in 1995. A Thai woman, Pharanee Deters, and her American ex-serviceman husband, Bill, who had worked in Vietnam, Thailand and Burma, had retired there to live a quieter, wildlife-centred life. Edwin admired them both.

A military man, Bill had many weapons in his house, and he employed many Burmese people to help run the property which included a rescue centre with more than 35 gibbons.

In May 2002, a 19-year-old Burmese man, Muang Htwe – Tui – who had recently quit under a cloud after working for four years at the centre, returned to steal the weapons from the house to sell over the Thai-Burmese border. There was big demand for such weapons and selling them was easy money. The teenager knew where the guns were kept and that there were several of them.

In his confession later, Tui claimed to have been caught by surprise to find Bill in the kitchen because he had expected him to be out as was his usual pattern at that time of day. He says he shot Bill dead in a panic, and then turned guns on the young cook and her three-year-old daughter, who was standing by her side and had said his name. There were two staff working outside, one constructing a guesthouse and one employed to do some welding and to feed the animals. They were next on the hit list. Each person was shot in the head with two different guns.

There was only one volunteer at Highland Farm at the time, 25-year-old Dutchman Bram Osterloh, who had been there less than a week. Bram was to work for Edwin for more than three years later on and told him what happened next. Bram fled to the second floor of the building but lost his glasses, which were vital for him to see properly. He took a knife and hid in the bathroom. The killer called to Bram from downstairs, saying he knew where he was. Bram moved to spots he hoped would be safe between the bathroom and the closet and saw a vehicle arrive during the night, presumably to take possession of the guns. Tui's two brothers were later sentenced to eight years' jail each for helping to sell the guns over the border.

Bram did not dare come down until the next morning. In the breaking light of day, he fled the house and flagged down a vehicle. The driver took him to the police. Later that morning, the police called Edwin, asking him to come and take care of the animals.

"The general, who was supervising the province and later became director of the forestry police, knew my work because we had been in contact before. He told me Bill was dead and a lot of others too, and that Bill's wife was in Bangkok. They said there are a lot of animals here and no one left to look after them," Edwin says. "I got into the car, took some clothing and my now ex-girlfriend and two volunteers and drove up. We got there after midnight. It was about a nine-hour drive, and the first thing that struck me was a lot of blood. There was brain matter and bone on the walls. It was very difficult to see.

"When I got there in the middle of the night, the team securing the scene were all drunk. There were four there and a Hummer with an automatic weapon on top. These things are seared in my mind."

The reason was ghosts; Thais are terrified of ghosts. In addition, the killer had not yet been caught. Bram was held in a police station in a cell because they were not sure whether he was perpetrator or victim.

"My girlfriend and the volunteers did not want to stay in the place looking like that. But I felt I had to be there. I got to the room and said I was going to stay, and the police said if I was staying, they would go. They talked about ghosts; they were scared. They gave me a gun and left the Hummer, and they took off.

"I went to one of the bedrooms and opened the door and looked down, and there was blood on the doorknob. There was blood on my hands – dried up already – but I was sweating and it had made the blood wet again and got stuck on my hands.

"Of course, the killer had been checking every room, looking for Bram. I found a bed; it was very late by now, and I had a disc player, and there was David Gray singing *Sail Away* in my ears.

I lay down, and there was something hard under my head. It was a hand gun, and I did not sleep at all the rest of the night."

At 5 am, the gibbons started singing, and the night was over. By 9 am, the first of the police and crime scene officials came, and the media arrived.

"It was one of the few nights in my life I will never forget; for the wrong reasons," Edwin says.

Tui was sentenced to death for the murders in early 2003.

"After the murders, our staff and volunteers continued to help at Highland Farm for another six months," he says. "We spent a lot of time and money on the care and support of those animals, and it is a long way away, so it was extremely disappointing to read in an English newspaper that Monkey World from the UK claimed to do all the work at the farm after the murder. Our volunteers were utterly alone and never saw them there. It was again a wake-up call that the biggest threat to our work came from within the animal sector."

Edwin and Pha's relationship was not to last, sacrificed on the altar of the illicit drugs that enslave so many in the district. The use of methamphetamine and similar drugs upcountry in Thailand is a massive problem.

Pha started by dabbling in the euphoric, exotic chemicals socially, but swiftly fell under their spell. Her disintegration was quick and dramatic as her chemical dependence became her driving force and getting high became her only objective. As with so many addicts, she became unreliable, untrustworthy and utterly self-focused. Edwin says he felt confused at first, then wanted to help Pha, but then he realised she did not want to be free of the drugs. He mourned the woman he had lost, but realised he could no longer be with her, and asked her to move out. But Nom stayed on.

He says now that in some ways, staying with Pha was a massive mistake of his life. Her drug problems marred his reputation by association within the community. Her erratic behaviour led to many misunderstandings.

For Edwin, it was a time for double endings, with all matters finally legally resolved between him and Noi. He got the result he expected: he was awarded nothing.

She had everything including the businesses, which were taken into liquidation two years later. And while being awarded zilch was a final slap, this also helped Edwin have a feeling of the decks having been cleared.

It was a blessing in disguise; he was finally free of all the remnants of his old life.

8. Feels like Heaven

At the Kao Luk Chang wildlife rescue centre, the rhythm of renewed life started beating powerfully.

As the rescue facility became known in the area, there were more callouts to retrieve kept wildlife. In the beginning, it was a refuge, and Edwin accepted that rescued pets had almost zero chance of being rehabilitated to the point of being able to survive in the wild. If an animal needed safe haven, Edwin and his team would take it in, crafting a suitable cage or enclosure as quickly as possible. They had to be nimble because the species and numbers varied day-to-day, and their stay might stretch for years.

Edwin says he was happy and liked the forward momentum that came with breathing life into his vision. He was comfortable with the set-up and felt secure that the toehold they built in a short time was becoming a stronger foothold.

And he soon had a partner to do it with.

In 2003, Edwin met Jansaeng Sangnanork, yet another Noi, when he was staying at his regular hotel on an overnighter in Bangkok. She was 25 and working there. Attractive and self-assured, her direct gaze and glossy black hair struck him; her oval face and rosebud mouth were beautiful. At the time, Noi had worked there for a short while as she sorted through the recent breakup of her marriage of two years. Edwin liked her strength and sense of self-direction.

Noi had worked in a Samsung factory for six years and with the financial settlement from her divorce, felt the niggle of a need for a big change. She had completed a short course at beauty school and then secured a job at the hotel, where two of her sisters had jobs. She had vague ideas of owning her own salon one day.

Noi could not have anticipated the whirlwind switch in direction that her life was about to take when she met the tall, blond Dutchman, who was 37 at the time. Within their first conversation, he told her he rescued and looked after wild animals.

"At first, I thought he was kind of interesting; he was quite good looking and talked in very good Thai, and I thought, *I want to see these monkeys that this crazy person looks after, one day,*" Noi says. "I would say I liked him 60 per cent, but I definitely thought he was a bit crazy, too."

They crossed paths a few more times, until finally Edwin asked her out. Their first date involved a rescue. Edwin said he needed to negotiate with some monks about taking a monkey from a temple near Bangkok. Noi had seen Edwin's truck before, and the idea of being part of a rescue excited her, even if she had no real knowledge about wild animals. The prospect of the outing was thrilling, and she watched as the monk and Edwin talked, noting how Edwin was both firm and polite in putting his case that the monkey's life would be better in his care. It was agreed that the monkey would not be surrendered that day, but that Edwin could come back to get it within the week.

Noi says she was struck by feeling sorry for the monkey on a chain, wondering why the monks wanted to keep it so confined and treat it in such a way. The reaction was foreign to her because she had never deeply considered the plight of the wild creatures on chains and in cages that are so prevalent in Thailand.

She says she had an overwhelming feeling that rescuing animals and offering them a chance at a better life was a very important job, that it was good that there was an organisation now doing that, and she felt admiration for Edwin.

"I remember saying I felt sorry for that monkey and that it seemed so unfair for him. Edwin said: 'welcome to my world'. He used those words," she says.

Afterwards, they had dinner at an Italian restaurant, and Edwin invited Noi to come on the next weekend to see his wildlife rescue centre. The first time Noi visited Edwin's home at Khao Luk Chang stands out like a beacon in her mind. She remembers thinking he lived in a hovel; his room was tiny, disorganised and quite dirty. By now at the centre, there were three volunteers, a cook and of course, the keeper, Nom. Additional room blocks – a cluster of simple rooms with concrete walls, a tin roof and shared bathroom – were under construction.

Food was prepared in the open, wall-less space at the front of the accommodation block.

The centre had other residents: about 30 monkeys, a paralysed pig called Flip, a crocodile, two bears, Friday and Kijke, and Edwin's beautiful tiger Meow.

When Edwin met her, Noi had already committed to improving her skills to increase her work opportunities. She had undertaken to learn computer skills and develop her English so that she perhaps might be able to gain work at the front desk at the hotel. She was soon not only spending workdays at work and evenings at school, but weekends at Edwin's, three hours' drive away. This was to be the rhythm of many weeks.

She says that when Edwin asked her to stay for good and make her life with him in Khao Luk Chang, she had to think it through carefully, having to convince herself it would be OK. She felt assured because he spoke such fluent Thai and believed so much in what he did, but it was a big leap of faith to leave her job and studies in Bangkok. She was hitching her wagon to a renegade and that is not the traditional Thai way.

But once the decision was made, she threw herself into the new life, going to the market to buy the animal food herself and helping Nom. She became involved in ordering supplies, loading goods on and off trucks, and she learnt conscientiously about animal care. It was a very long way from her childhood in a rice farming family in north eastern Thailand.

"I had never thought about being with a European man before, and if he had not spoken very good Thai, I would not have been interested in him because we would not have talked like we did," she says. "But pretty soon I felt I loved him and wanted to be with him. And I wanted to help the animals, and he made me feel like I could do something good. I felt I was useful, that I could do something to help him, and also that he needed my help."

From the start of their partnership, Edwin would take Noi along on rescues, and she proved herself to have a calm head and a useful set of hands. That she has a strong disposition and is not often a wildly emotional person helped in circumstances that were often tricky and complicated. Having a Thai woman present was also sometimes the final dose of encouragement an animal keeper needed to surrender their creature.

"I was not scared even though I did not know much about animals," she says. "If I was with him in a relationship, I thought that I had to automatically be a part of that. But I got used to it, and that he loved the animals and felt strongly about them having better lives was enough for me to join him. I also think I was helpful to him by giving him moral support and someone to talk to."

Foreigners in Thailand cannot own land. Without a great deal of loophole finding, they cannot head Thai companies or organisations. Even after almost three decades in Thailand, Edwin's life must still feature a planned, regular cycle of visa renewals.

Noi spent two years on university studies during the early years with Edwin but had little time for it and failed to complete her degree. Despite the lack of the piece of parchment, she had knowledge of business and management practices in Thailand. Noi found that Edwin did not have a proper office system in place, so she developed a structure to keep track of rescues and record each animal's needs and the care they received. Then, as now, the system was paper-based, as it is in most of Thailand. But order and speed in their paperwork system was neither a focus nor a strength for Edwin or Noi – their prime motivator was the animals and their care – and that was to cause them some grief later.

The government requires registration of rescued animals, which starts with going to a police station or a government department and logging the incident. But on occasion, an animal might be in care for only a day or two, perhaps with just a minor injury that just needs patching before its release back into the wild, and Noi says they would hold off to see whether it was worth creating a file for a temporary visitor.

In the circumstances of WFFT rescuing an injured animal, the focus is always on the animal first, not meeting the official requirements. Both Edwin and Noi are clear about that. The call-out might come in the middle of the night or to a location far from a police station or official's office. In those cases, doing a double drive to lodge the registration would be needed and was not always possible.

And as in all matters of life in Thailand, many rules are unwritten and others are not uniformly enforced.

The couple settled into a kind of wild rhythm. The variation in each day made it exciting. Noi says she realised she felt more settled and happier with Edwin than she had been in her adult life, and even though she and Edwin have never married, she considers she became his wife in 2003.

"There is a perception that if you have a foreigner husband, you are really rich and do not have to work hard – that he will look after you and you just look after the house," she says. "But I work very hard – we work hard. My family saw that from the start. It is not what it looks like to people from a distance: we have always worked very, very hard."

Noi was also a good match for Edwin, as she was quite independent and did not demand his constant attention. She may well have been the perfect fit for one who is always on the move and in need of challenges, for this newly-minted wildlife warrior.

Edwin admits he finds big events exciting and gets an adrenalin surge from them. He has never been one to run away when trouble has knocked and is quick to dive in to a situation, however dangerous, when he feels he has something to offer.

Early on Boxing Day, 2004, an undersea megathrust earthquake occurred, with the epicentre off the west coast of Sumatra. It triggered a series of devastating tsunamis that hit along the coasts of the adjoining landmasses, delivering waves up to 30m high and killing as many as 280,000 people in 14 nations. Thailand was one of the nations hit worst. Edwin says that on Boxing Day, a TV report said there had been a giant wave at Phuket and soon after that, there was talk that 20 or 30 people may have drowned in it.

"We had never heard of a tsunami. We had no real idea of what that meant. The information and news was not as quick then, because there was no Twitter or Facebook," Edwin says. "Then we heard that maybe there were more than 50 dead and that some other countries had been affected, too."

Edwin took a call from someone he knew closer to Phuket, who said maybe Edwin should come down and lend a hand because there were countless injured people and maybe some animals were in need of help, too.

"Of course, I had to go. I have to be in the middle of things, and I did not hesitate to make the nine-hour drive," he says.

"About 12 of us went in three cars, and we took dog food and some supplies. Of course, we found devastation that we could not have imagined. It was horrible and people were not just dead, but many bodies had been terribly damaged. But we found there was not a lot to be done because those animals and people who were dead, were dead. But then we heard that things were much worse in the north in Khao Lak, about 100km north of Phuket."

The WFFT team arrived to find that more than 4000 people had died there. They helped with moving debris and signalling where bodies were to be found, pitching in without much of a system.

"But then we started hearing about dolphins being stuck in a tin mine that was about two miles in from the coast. At first, it was thought there were a few, but it turned out to be one," he says. "There is usually just a bit of water in the mine, which is very deep, but as this big wave came in, it filled the whole thing. The scale of this wave was hard to find words for. A lot of people had been dragged into the mine and had been pulled out again.

"But as well as the people, the wave had carried in a pink dolphin, an Indo-Pacific humpback dolphin. They are rare, and quite beautiful to look at with their stunning, smooth pink skin. By then, the mine was a lake."

The dolphin was large and clearly distressed. Edwin, his team and a huge number of locals set about trying to catch the dolphin in order to get it back into the right body of water.

"She was very stressed and very dehydrated. We could see she had had a tough time and had been beaten about by the trip inland; she had a lot of wounds in need of treatment. Dolphins do not drink, but are hydrated by the fish they eat, so she was rapidly deteriorating," Edwin says. "We knew we had to catch her quickly, and lucky for us she had to come up for air and was bright pink, so we could see at most times where she was within the body of water."

It took three frustrating days to catch the dolphin by slowly driving her into a corner and holding her there by using a long, deep net. Twice she leapt over the top of the net and they had to repeat the process. A lot of local people came to help and to watch.

"It was a positive story in the middle of a terrible lot of misery," Edwin says. "It made the news all over the world."

The Prime Minister Thaksin Shinawatra got involved after seeing the story on TV and wanted to hold the dolphin up as a symbol of survival amid such dreadful devastation. It was reported that Thaksin wanted to put the dolphin in an aquarium at Phuket so that tourists could come and see it. The Minister of the Department of Natural Resources Suwit Khunkitty then weighed in.

"I have never seen a man so dedicated to helping in a real way," Edwin says. "Suwit Khunkitty was at the morgue at the temple, as all the dead bodies were being piled up, talking to families and offering emotional support. Bodies were being identified by Australian and Dutch and French officials and police forensic experts, and this minister could not have been more dedicated or compassionate."

The minister came by helicopter to the site of the dolphin rescue.

"He whispered to us 'I think if you have treated the wounds and force fed it, and if you think it is strong enough, you should put it back into the sea. That would be much better for the dolphin'."

Edwin had never rescued a dolphin before and took advice from experts on how to get the right nutrients into her. The wounds were tended and the military helped them get her to the ocean.

They put a ribbon on her tail to be sure she could be recognised in the crucial, initial days, telling everyone it was a pink ribbon, when really it was a blue one as Thai people are renowned for telling a person in authority what they want to hear.

"But then one day, a fisherman said he had not seen one dolphin with a pink ribbon, but had seen one in a group with a blue one. We knew then that she had made it, that she was fine."

The rescue continues to be one Edwin is proud of, and he has never heard what the Prime Minister's reaction was to the dolphin's release. But it was also an early warning shot for Edwin, with others claiming the glory for the rescue.

"Humane Society International and World Society for the Protection of Animals claimed to be helping," Edwin says. "They did not help me in any way. They were making photographs as we were doing the rescue, and the photos were spectacular because she really was something to see. We did not have time for making photos or telling people what we were doing because we were busy with trying to save her. We were doing, and they were photographing and pretending they were doing. I was shocked that they would act in this way. I felt they screwed us. It was shockingly bad."

Edwin later complained to the organisations that they had not given WFFT credit where it was due. After a bit of to and fro, the Humane Society donated a dinghy with a little outboard engine to WFFT as an apology. WSPA donated $US10,000 to WFFT, which was used to start the building of a proper medical facility for wildlife at the centre.

The first medical unit, the Observation and Recovery Unit, had been built behind the volunteer house at the wildlife rescue centre in about 2003. Three cages with a side enclosure were next to a little table and a sink, where animals could be cleaned up, preliminarily treated and then taken to a vet if necessary.

The introduction of a mini-clinic was necessary because people had begun to call WFFT when wild animals were injured. Some just needed a quick fix and could be released rapidly back into the area where they were found. Some needed months of care and some could never live in the wild again.

On the early call-outs to an injured animal, Edwin or one of his staff would sedate it and take it to the nearest veterinary surgery, and they would pay the vet. Edwin was always good with a gun – a remnant of his military days – and found darting with a blow pipe easy too, so sedation was not an issue. With the growth in animal numbers came an increased need for vet care on the campus, and taking wild animals to available vets could be a problem as well. Edwin recalls once having to drive Meow in his open pick-up truck to a vet in Petchaburi for an x-ray.

"That was a weird situation, and I have to admit I found myself in them a few times where you stop at a traffic light and get these looks from people, staring at this tiger in the back," Edwin says. "And then you pull up and park in the middle of the city, and four people are pulling a tiger off the bed of a truck. I would not do it now, but at the time, that was the only way we thought we could get the right help."

It was soon clear that a better-equipped clinic was needed.

Towards the end of 2004, the first proper clinic was started. Edwin employed a veterinary nurse to run the place, and a unit with three cages and the possibility for two of the animals to go outside was constructed. There was an office, a sink and a stainless steel surgery table in the middle, lit well. It was 24 square metres, a tiny space, but it was air conditioned which was quite radical at the time. It was to be the centre's hospital until 2008.

WFFT's centre was an oasis in the tough landscape of the region. The work done and the animals within the perimeter gained some attention, and it attracted volunteers who wanted to be a part of one of the only refuges in the world that was focused on encouraging animals to be animals, rather than tamed house pets. The daily work for volunteers comprised mainly cleaning enclosures and preparing food for the animals and, at times, undertaking special projects to keep the place growing to accommodate increasing numbers of new arrivals.

It was gritty, tough but satisfying routine. There was a steady stream of people who wanted to do it.

But then Edwin was offered an opportunity that would see the centre boom: elephants.

They are loved the world over for allegedly never forgetting, for being wise and for having an appealing balance of fire and cool. Their family loyalties and social interactions within their group fascinate all kinds of people globally. Elephants have a special place in Thai culture. They are the symbol of the nation and are admired for their toughness, their hard work and their stoicism. The King of Thailand has a Royal Elephant Stable of 10 revered "white" elephants. They are long living and trainable, their sheer size earning them a place in history for working under human instruction in logging, transporting and earth shifting endeavours, stretching back eons to the time before mechanisation revolutionised industries.

Domesticated elephants are also used and abused in Thailand in ways that the West is increasingly finding unpalatable. In Thailand, domesticated elephants are property, much like a dog or cat or a cow. They are not considered wildlife.

Currently, there are estimated to be about 3000 domesticated elephants in the country and most of these work in the tourism industry including trekking camps, carrying tourists in an arduous, relentless pattern for long days. Their conditions are often deplorable, with the sharp edge of a bull hook dictating the speed and direction of their movements, no chance to walk freely or interact with others, limited access to water and a restricted diet. The welfare and living standards are almost always far below the benchmarks expected in the West.

The use of the term 'domesticated' confuses some as it implies these are a different strain from the diminishing numbers of pachyderms that live in the forested areas of the national parks. But there is no genetic or behavioural difference between them, meaning domesticated elephants are captive wild elephants by another name. Most of the elephants that are currently working were definitely taken as babies from the wild because there was very little breeding of elephants in Asia until the 1990s.

In 1989, the Thai Government banned all logging in protected areas, effectively closing all remaining natural forests. While all conservationists agreed this was a positive, necessary, forward-thinking move, its side effect was that it threw logging elephants out of work. This coincided with a surge in international tourists flocking to a more receptive, open Thailand, and the logging elephants serviced a surge in demand to give visitors the thrill of a ride aloft on a magnificent beast, sitting in a basket as she stomped her massive feet slowly along a well-worn track and all for a few hundred baht.

But it is known now that the price the animal pays is far greater. After decades of service with never a day to rest, they are likely to have spinal problems from carrying ill-fitting baskets stuffed with several people. They develop infections and irritations in the folds of their wrinkled, tough skin. Many have vision problems due to ill treatment or diabetes due to the wrong nutrition. In the worst of the camps, they are beaten and carry wounds from that too, and their problems are not addressed. These elephants are simply abandoned or left to languish when they can no longer walk and therefore are unable to earn their keepers a wage.

Edwin would like to see the use and abuse of elephants for tourist entertainment end, but he also must keep a toe in the water because he needs to stay abreast of the goings on in that industry. Edwin is naturally a curious person and loves to look behind the curtains to glean first-hand information about all manner of animal issues.

"I do not have a good relationship with the elephant camps. I never have had," Edwin says. "I have been threatened, and they have said some horrible things about me. I sat in a meeting at Parliament a couple of weeks ago, and they told the officials there that I am pretending to be a wildlife conservationist and wildlife carer. They told the meeting the only reason I do what I do is because I make big money out of it. That is what they say to my face. So no, I have never had and never will have any kind of a relationship with them, except a bad one.

"But the thing is that I understand them far better than they think. I have quite a mild opinion of what should happen to these elephant camps, but they do not stop long enough to hear that. I am very interested in finding alternatives to trekking in the way it continues to be done. I don't want them instantly shut down because that stops the income those people need, and it puts a whole lot of elephants on the streets."

In 2004, Edwin was struggling to attract enough volunteers to run the burgeoning centre; the labour needed to care for so many diverse species was not being matched by the number of volunteers applying to come. Edwin had visited three and researched other elephant sanctuaries and seen that people's fascination with elephants drew them in with volunteers lining up to work with these giant beasts. It was a human resource and income stream that Edwin wanted a slice of.

"I did not have the money to buy an elephant and also I did not want to give these people so much money, because that can feed the market and therefore the problem of elephants being taken from the wild, something I abhor. But I strongly felt that I could have an ethically run refuge for elephants, which would make money and that the money could therefore fund the rescuing of other wildlife.

"I thought to myself, *This is what we need; this is what we are going to do.* I just had to work out how to make it happen."

Edwin knew a man involved in an elephant camp near the Bangkok floating market who was looking to open a new camp, and Edwin suggested instead of a camp, he could come to a kind of radical arrangement with him at the Khao Luk Chang rescue centre. Instead of loading the elephants up with heavy baskets to give rides to paying guests, the elephants could still draw people, but live freer lives.

Edwin offered 12,000 baht per month for each of the elephants.

"Looking back at it, he had a good deal, but I also had a good deal, and the elephants had the best deal," Edwin says. "They would still be chained at night in those days because we did not have enclosures or space for them for another two to three years. But they were happy, and we were able to control things like their treatment at the hands of the mahouts and also others."

Three elephants and their mahouts came to live at the centre. Nam Fon, Soy Thong and Kiew Ta had each had years of service, and Edwin saw this as a chance to give them a better daily life and an opportunity to regain their health in their later years.

For the first six months, the mahouts stayed in tents on the grounds, but once the income from increased volunteer numbers started coming in, Edwin built a mahout house in which they could each have a room. It still stands today.

The abbot was pleased to have elephants on the temple land and locals were warned that the rescue centre now had elephants, so to be careful in the area at night. During the day, in essence, the elephants roamed on the grounds, sometimes sharing the space with cows. Eventually, more land was given and enclosures for the elephants were built.

Edwin had a loose agreement that he would buy the elephants when he had the money, but when he periodically revisited this, the owner kept jacking the price up. There were other problems, too. One of the mahouts was an alcoholic, and Edwin became aware he was using methamphetamines, and the double troubles made him a particular danger around animals. After a while, the arrangement broke down and the mahouts left in the middle of one night in 2010. Nam Fon, Soy Thong and Kiew Ta were put back to work in trekking camps, lugging tourists.

Edwin vowed never to rent an elephant again, and to be sure each of the pachyderms at the refuge could not be removed on a human whim. That way, he could promise them assuredly that they were safe and could never be forced to work again.

Nam Fon was to come back to the WFFT elephant refuge in 2016, her freedom bought this time with money from a kind donor and her security assured. She died at the centre by the water in January 2017. Her WFFT mahout Aek says in his dreams, he still walks with her in the forest.

Kiew Ta was killed in 2016 when the truck in which she was being transported from one elephant camp to another suddenly hit the brakes. She was unsecured and fell heavily in the body of the vehicle, causing ultimately fatal injuries.

Soy Thong was seen in 2017 in a trekking camp, pregnant and working.

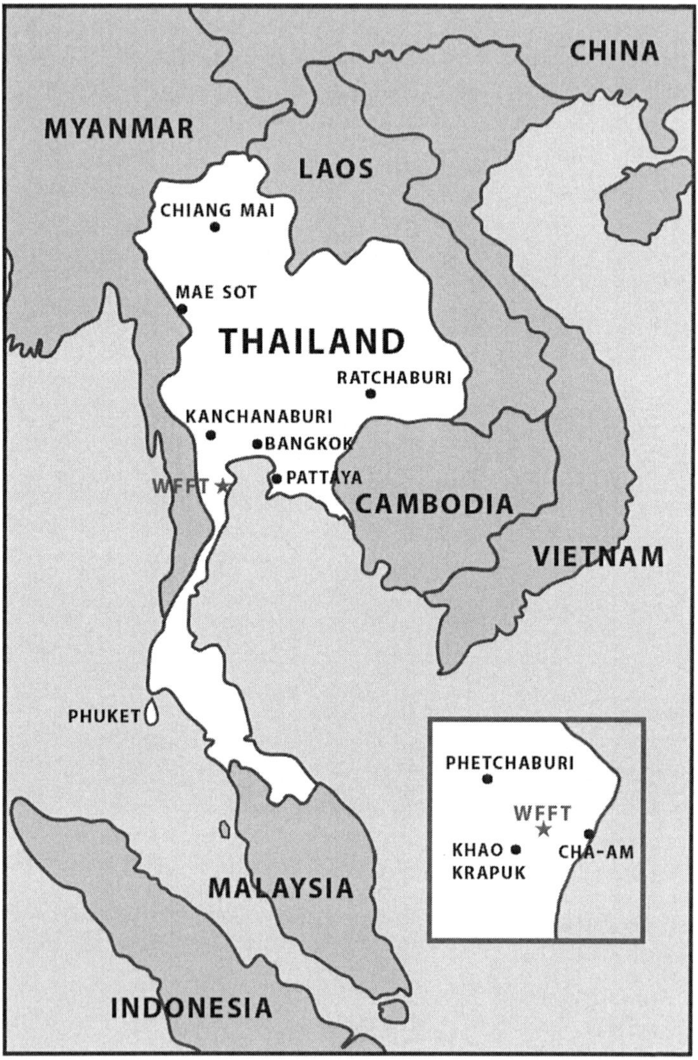
CHINA
MYANMAR
LAOS
CHIANG MAI
MAE SOT
THAILAND
RATCHABURI
KANCHANABURI
BANGKOK
WFFT
PATTAYA
CAMBODIA
VIETNAM
PHUKET
MALAYSIA
INDONESIA
PHETCHABURI
WFFT
KHAO KRAPUK
CHA-AM

Edwin works on the tsunami dolphin rescue, 2004

Edwin and Noi in Europe, 2008

Edwin with a little rescue, 2009

Edwin with Meow, 2010

Edwin addresses a government
assembly on the dog meat trade, 2013

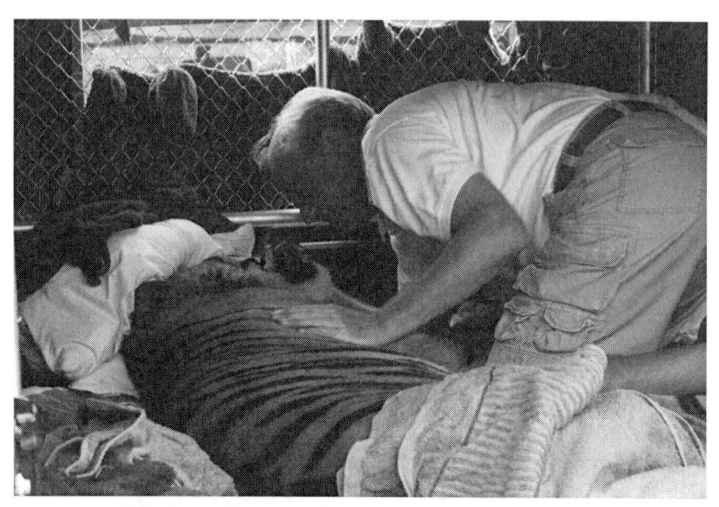

Edwin and Meow just before the tiger's death

Edwin and Noi outside the court, 2014

A Buddhist blessing for WFFT 2015

Edwin with one of the shipments of orangutans he helped
repatriate to Indonesia

Joan Pearson

Tommy Taylor

Edwin with baby langur

9. That's What Friends Are For

Wartime British Prime Minister Winston Churchill said the price for greatness is responsibility, and for Edwin, this weighs heavily. For years, it has disturbed his sleep and caused him daytime worry. He also learnt the tough truth of US general Colin Powell's assertion: "Being responsible sometimes means pissing people off."

"One of the reasons I do not have children is that I do not think I can hold that responsibility," he says. "Whether legally I hold it or not, I feel personally responsible when things go wrong. And in many ways, I have very great difficulty taking personal credit for when things go well.

"We had a bear escape from its enclosure a few days ago, and from the moment I heard it until the moment it was back in, I had the worst-case scenario going through my head. I worried about the bear, and I worried about my staff and volunteers. I know logically that nearly always, everything will work out without anything terrible happening as the staff are well trained for these emergencies, but it is sometimes like my mind has its own agenda: to keep me on the edge and my forehead creased."

After the first four or five years of WFFT, the wildlife rescue centre and elephant refuge were expanding, and its practises deepening, and with that came more staff, more volunteers and more animals to care for. By 2007, there were 250 animals on 16ha of land, and the variety was stunning. People had surrendered a menagerie that featured everything from bears and civets to langur and gibbons, macaques and otters, deer and a leopard. By now, Edwin had employed 24 people to help run the operation and direct the swelling numbers of volunteers.

Many of the animals carried permanent disabilities or injuries. Bouncer, an Asiatic black bear, almost died when his leg was caught in a trap set by a poacher in Kaeng Krachan

National Park in 2004. He is a happy, handsome WFFT resident, his three-legged lumbering serving him very well in a wide-open field.

Bandit, a long-tailed macaque, was born at Kao Wang in Petchaburi with no legs and just one arm. A caring local brought her as a little baby to WFFT, knowing she has no chance of survival in the wild. Bandit was raised by a foster mother and has found a place within a cobbled-together family of macaques in an open field. She gets around remarkably well using her one arm, rallying at food time and playing and interacting normally with her adopted family. The volunteers affectionately call her Potato, a salute to her somewhat bulbous, startlingly truncated appearance.

In starting WFFT, Edwin says he realised he would have to take others along with him, that he could never do what he needed to for the animals without many helping hands and like-minded heads. And while the hands came to him in increasing numbers from the volunteering international community and also from the local village and surrounds, finding a shared ethos even within the animal welfare sector proved more difficult.

"I respect anyone who is helping animals, who are working in this field, but the way they do things is different," Edwin says. "Some of them have enclosures that are far too small; many are too hands-on for my liking.

"But there are some places I have bigger issues with. In Thailand, it is far too easy to buy a couple of elephants and call yourself a rescue centre or an animal sanctuary. There are people who are nuts, and there are people who own their centres personally and have not set it up as a foundation. By foundation I mean they set it up for the greater good, for the animals, in a sustainable way rather than for their own profit as a business. That, I have a problem with. And there are many of them."

Edwin says while he has gratefully received long-standing support from International Primate Protection League in the UK, he has rarely been the beneficiary of financial support from big NGO animal welfare and conservation organisations such as World Animal Protection or the International Fund for Animal Welfare.

"I have asked them to help us in the past, and they basically do not even reply," he says. "But what pisses me off is that when something is in the news and we do good work, they immediately speak and praise the work or the improvement. They use our stories, our work and our photos, and they ask for donations to themselves. I have no respect for that.

"When you spend more than 60 per cent of your income on maintaining the salaries for staff and your public relations department, then logically, less than 40 per cent is going to the animals. Here, our overhead is about 17-18 per cent, and that is how it should be. I think there should be international guidelines on NGOs around the amount of money they should designate for overheads."

Edwin sees his business model as sensible and sustainable. The iron-clad policy is that any development within the Foundation will not be started without the funding for it having been secured. Credit is avoided at all costs. Edwin also knew that from the start, he wanted to help rescued animals re-find some of their instincts, regardless of how long they had been captive. At WFFT, the elephants are unchained; it is believed to be the only completely chain-free centre in Thailand, and all other animals are hands-off to volunteers. His aim and expectations are that the animal welfare standards are the highest in any Asian wildlife rescue facility.

Those in the West who rescue abused and abandoned dogs, cats and other animals lavish them with love and affection, restoring their trust in humans by giving them security in a human home. But Edwin chooses to rescue and rehabilitate animals because they are wild or because he believes they should be. The ultimate for him is when a rescued animal behaves in the opposite way to trusting and depending on a human; he wants them wild and free, exhibiting behaviours that do not require human approval, affection or interaction. They may be reliant on people for safety and food, but he feels happiest when they interact with each other and exhibit wild behaviours instead of taught ones.

"For example, the stump tailed macaques will groom each other. They will interact. They will have a balanced, co-operative group life," he says. "One could reason that in many ways the animals at our centre that live in the open enclosures have a better life than they would in the wild because they have no predators, no hunters, and they do not have to stress about finding food because we ensure they get enough."

Ultimately, Edwin does not want the animals to need him. He wants them to need each other.

While Edwin has struggled to find support and like minds within the animal conservation sector, other supporters have found him, sometimes in the most unexpected ways.

Of all those who have backed Edwin in his work, Joan Pearson from Sydney, Australia is a standout. No individual has done more financially or offered greater moral support than she has. In animal welfare circles in Australia, Joan is known and admired. Her fundraising in Sydney for a broad range of animal charities is renowned and achieves extraordinary results. Joan was awarded an Order of Australia Medal in 2014 for her work in raising money for animal welfare organisations. Recipient charities have included those concerned with the welfare of chimps, bears, elephants, rhino, dogs and cats and Australian wildlife. The praise for her fundraising was something of a surprise to her.

"I have always liked to work hard," Joan says. "I have never very much liked time on my hands, and it's nice to be able to give back to something that needs it. Animals need us; so many could not survive without our help."

Torture and bad treatment of animals, more than anything else, upset this lithe, blonde dynamo. But instead of being paralysed by sadness, she uses her seemingly boundless energy to do something practical about it. Joan is about far more than simply fundraising; she uses her personal time and elbow grease to turn animal horror stories into happy endings.

"I get very upset about what people do to animals. Sometimes I feel angry, but mostly, I just have this feeling that I want to do something to alleviate their situation," she says. "I am negotiating at the moment about getting an elephant at the moment in Pattaya, for example. I saw her for myself.

"She is blind in one eye and has these scars over the top with open wounds in addition, and every time she has people on her back, the mahout was sticking the bull hook into the wounds and the sore spots. It was utterly disgusting."

Joan, 73, is steely. When she goes to Asia, she visits the dirty corners that few animal activists have the stomach to even peer into. She goes into camps and farms, and despite witnessing abuses at human hands that revolt her, she uses that experience to identify those individual creatures most in need and also to strengthen her resolve to help them.

"I come back to Sydney, and I get excited because I know it is that *particular* elephant that I will be helping. That excitement catches on a little bit because I can describe that specific elephant or animal to my friends; I can tell that particular story. If people can connect with an animal with that story, they are more likely to be motivated to help."

In 2006, Joan and her friend from Sydney, Val Scott, were on their way back to Sydney after 10 days with 'Free the Bears' in Cambodia and found themselves with an unencumbered day in Bangkok. Neither woman likes idle time and both are animal crazy. Joan had heard about and researched WFFT before their trip and suggested they make the trip three hours southwest to take a look for themselves. That decision was to change the face of WFFT.

"We had a good look around, and then we had a sandwich, and I had a talk with Edwin," she says. "I liked what he was doing there. It felt right. I could see he was someone who, when he says he will do something, generally does it. I liked that there was compassion there at the centre too. I felt that the people there really cared, and I knew that if I donated money, he would use it in the right way."

In 2006, Joan and her then-husband Martin gave Edwin money to buy two elephants: Martin paid for Pai Lin and Joan for Somboon. They were the first elephants to be owned by WFFT.

Pai Lin, who had a life of begging on the streets after being discharged because years of work in a trekking camp had deformed her spine, arrived at the centre by truck in February, 2007. She was then thought to be aged about 60. Somboon, who was probably 15 years younger, had been working the streets of Suphanburi when she was hit by a car in 2006 and hurt badly enough to leave her with a permanent limp. She arrived at WFFT in April, 2007.

But Joan had bigger plans. There was to be an art show at a gallery in Sydney, showing the animal-themed works of Richard Allen, a contemporary Australian artist. The gallery thought Joan might like to use the space as a venue for a dinner to raise funds for one of her animal charities. WFFT was to be her target.

The evening raised $A74,000, more than any amount the seasoned fundraiser had raised in one night before or since. Edwin was floored by the donation which was the largest single lump sum the Foundation had ever received.

Joan had been raising funds for animal charities since 2001, when she had the first fundraising meal at her harbour side home for World Animal Day at the suggestion of World Society for the Protection of Animals. Her guests were asked to bring their own chairs that time, because Joan simply did not have enough. Now she has a well-worn system in place and her dinners, which also feature an auction and raffles, have become renowned; at one point, they were held monthly, and she has had up to 130 people to cook and cater for. Most are held in her beautiful harbour side home. She has an extensive list of people on her invitation list and every cent raised goes to charity. The annual WFFT dinners raise about $A50,000 in a single evening. The donations go to Humane Society International, so that even though WFFT does not have an Australian registration, they can be tax deductible for the donor. HSI then ensures the money reaches its target.

Born in South Africa, Joan moved to Australia with her family when she was 13, and her mother died a year later. She says, despite having to accommodate such a massive loss in a new land, the move to Australia was the best thing ever to happen to her. She was accepted at Queenwood School, and there she felt valued and supported. She loved every bit of it, and she says it set her up to feel confident and capable in the adult years to come.

"I have had a blessed life," Joan says. "I really like people, and I feel very grateful to have such a broad circle of friends, because through the dinners those who might not have known each other are now friends, too. But I have also seen what some people are capable of doing to the animals, and I have to say that if a person has no passion for animals, much less abuses them, they are not a person I would choose to associate with. It is as simple as that to me because those people who have no time for animals are totally selfish."

Joan and Edwin have become firm friends. He says he thinks of her as his second mother, and she is one of few people who can tell him frankly when she thinks he is out of line without him exploding in response. Their banter is refreshing, and the comfort they feel with each other is plain. Edwin talks to her regularly on the phone and bounces ideas for WFFT developments and improvements off her. He visits Sydney each year to attend Joan's WFFT fundraising dinner and stays for a week with her in her waterside home. Such breaks from the coalface of brutal hours and high conflict world are rare and Joan loves Noi, too.

In all, Joan and her supporters have paid for more than 20 elephants. They have also paid for the land on which the only fully-equipped elephant hospital in the region sits. Each elephant is a precious life to Joan and offering an individual elephant refuge and a better existence makes her feel like she is making a small but important difference.

"Sometimes the prices are just too high," Joan says. "Sometimes they just make too much money for their owner in the tourist trade, and the owner won't want to give it up. In those cases, I have to let it go, but it is heart-breaking, really. You can want all you like but you can't always make it happen, no matter how much you wish it."

Joan has facilitated the raising of about $1 million for WFFT. She visits the rescue centre and elephant refuge at least once a year. She says nothing gives her greater joy than the elephants that she has paid for having a secure and easy life, but she is also always keen to get home to Sydney to the numerous dogs and cats she fosters.

For Joan, there is always another animal to save or animal cause to support.

She observes, somewhat bitter sweetly, that need is never ending.

In 2008, another person who was to become intrinsic at WFFT arrived at the Khao Luk Chang centre. Tommy Taylor, a rangy, outgoing 20-year-old Englishman, came as a volunteer, fresh from heartbreak in Australia. He had a fiery passion for animals and a desire to make a practical difference in some way and threw himself into the relentless volunteering rhythm. He stayed for six months.

How far he has come: today, he is the director of the Foundation's wildlife rescue centre, co-ordinating and ever-improving animal care and overseeing enclosure design. He is also Edwin's right-hand man, and as deputy director, he is one of a handful of people whose opinion Edwin values when decisions need to be made. They are firm friends as well as a strong executive team, despite being polar opposites in almost every way. But they have in common a wicked sense of humour, a fierce work ethic and a deep desire to continually improve the animal welfare and enclosures at WFFT.

Tommy says he was always going to work with animals, but his volunteering experience consolidated the desire for professional involvement in wildlife conservation. It was also a whole lot of fun and gave him a great sense of belonging.

"There were two staff co-ordinating the volunteers and about 20 to 30 volunteers when I first came, so it was a really close-knit group, mostly from Europe," he says. "Honestly, I just loved the whole experience, the work with the animals and the bonds with the other volunteers, and I began to wonder if I was going to be able to settle back into regular life."

But the desire to build towards a stronger foothold that might help him be a part of a better future for animals was strong, and Tommy left the centre to accept a place at the University of Salford in Manchester to study wildlife and practical conservation. The decision was invigorating but settling back into regular English life after the steam and recklessness of Thailand also terrified him. It was a false start.

"In many ways, it was absolutely right for me. I felt studying in that field would give me the theory to go with the six months of practical experience I had at WFFT," he says. "I could seek work in the sector that I knew I belonged in. I then got a cryptic email from one of the staff, Simon Purser, which in essence said they wanted to hire an assistant volunteer co-ordinator and would I be interested.

"So, of course, I came back, happily and gratefully. It felt like the right thing to do, and I had made some very good friends, including Lucy Clark, who was a vet nurse here at the time. I felt very happy to delay the big step up."

Tommy stayed at WFFT for two-and-a-half years, and shifted into the volunteer co-ordinator role in that time. That duration is a relatively long tenure at the centre for a role that is constant and unforgiving. Dealing with the weekly churn of volunteers from all over the world coming and going, dealing with their needs and matching their labours to the animal requirements, plus the pressure of managing the weekly rosters, is a constant juggle. The rescue centre and refuge staff at WFFT work and live together, and their workdays start at dawn and have no real end. They get a single day off each week.

In January 2011, Tommy had a near-fatal motorbike crash at the village temple close to the rescue centre, leaving him with a badly broken clavicle, a fractured skull and a brain haemorrhage. Remarkably, he stayed on at WFFT through his recovery and returned to his job; such is the strength of his remarkable spirit. It was an accident he now rarely talks about in detail, but he carries shadows of it within him. He is a smart, compassionate and informed man.

"Throughout my teen years and early 20s, I campaigned and protested and was aggravated by animal cruelty. I would get highly emotional and frustrated," he says. "It didn't fizzle away, but the more abuse videos you see, the less actively affected you get. As I grow older, that is one of the positive effects of dealing with damaged and abused animals; I can turn off that part of myself in order to deal with certain horrors. It is the only way I can keep working in this space.

"I am not affected by every little thing anymore. If I were, I would be paralysed. It is training, I guess, but every now and then I am affected unexpectedly. I guess I would be a heartless bastard if I weren't."

Tommy is well informed about animal behaviour, welfare and needs. He is interesting to talk to, gregarious and fun, and it is a joy for others to be in his company. But he can be ferocious, too, particularly when it comes to wildlife.

"It has moved from the 'I want to murder you or at least stab you in the eye, you bastard, because I just watched you beat an elephant' response to the bigger picture. I see that clearly now. It sits in my mind when I see brutality, the need to stay separate and rational. I guess you could say I love and am concerned for animals, but I am in no way a bunny hugger."

Tommy resigned from WFFT to finally take up his place at the university in Manchester to study a Bachelor of Practical and Wildlife Conservation, leaving Thailand in February 2012. He graduated with excellent results in 2015, and his final project was a study of the social interaction of Barbary macaques.

He returned on September 1, 2015, this time as Edwin's second-in-charge.

Now in his middle years, Edwin accepts he has always had a predilection for trouble and conflict. It draws him in and, given it is not in his nature to ever be a simple bystander, he often becomes woven into the unfolding drama. That primal urge was stirred in May 2010 when political unrest again boiled over in the heart of Bangkok. And while Thailand is no stranger to political tumult, having had 18 coups, 23 military governments and almost a dozen military-dominated governments since the end of absolute monarchist control in 1932, this upheaval was particularly savage.

After days of protests on the greasy, steamy streets, protesters were warned that the authorities had had enough of central Bangkok being choked and disrupted. Armed forces would be moving in to clean them and their disruption out and restore life to order. The media covering the protests, including Edwin's friend Dutch TV journalist Michel Maas, who was based in Jakarta but covered all major Asian events, were braced for what was sure to be ensuing action. Edwin had spoken to Michel in the morning, so when Noi called Edwin at 11 am to tell him Michel had been shot in the back, he was shocked. A Japanese journalist had been shot dead, but Michel had survived and TV coverage showed him being taken to hospital on a motorbike, clearly severely injured.

Knowing his fluent Thai would be useful and fearful for his friend, Edwin chose to walk into the line of fire. Taking a rescue vehicle with lights and medical signage on it; it might have been for animals, but he reasoned that it might help him slip through the barricades to gain quicker access; he stepped into the fray, thinking at the very least he could help Michel get in touch with his wife and his media outlet to get his story out.

Edwin was stopped at checkpoints, but he talked his way through, saying he was there on official orders to help the injured foreigners. At the police hospital where Michel had been taken, he told the obstructing security guards he was Edwin Maas, brother of Michel Maas, who was upstairs. They let him in, but then he was faced with a fresh challenge; Michel told Edwin he needed items from his room at the Amari Watergate Hotel, which was across town. Edwin decided to run the gauntlet, but by now anarchy had ensued outside. Windows were being broken, cars and buildings were alight, and the military was strafing the crowd with bullets with armed militia returning fire.

"Part way there, I was being shot at from above as I zigzagged and dodged my way through the streets," Edwin says. "I had this thought, *What the fuck am I doing?* but it was just as far to go back as forward. I might be stupid or reckless or just have a hunger for trouble, but I decided I needed to see this through to its finish."

The next day, Edwin helped to extract Michel and get him to a better hospital. Michel made a full recovery and continues to work from Jakarta. He and Edwin remain good friends.

Considering his propensity for action and his avidly hands-on approach to life generally and the care of animals specifically, Edwin has had a remarkably unscathed run. Certainly, a few bruises and scrapes and the occasional need for stitches are all part of dealing with wild animals in his daily work. He acts on his extensive knowledge of their behaviour and has a way with them that commands them to offer him respect. He is warm but careful, never forgetting they are at their core uninhibited survivalists. But on December 1, 2012, he thought one of his cherished elephants would bring about his end.

At about 11 am that day, the small Thai female vet had to do an enema on Boonmee, an elderly elephant who had formerly had a life of working in logging and trekking camps but had been bought by Joan and her supporters. Boonmee had arrived at WFFT a month earlier, but she had been constipated for four days, and there were concerns for her health.

Edwin was involved in corralling her into a squeeze chute (similar to a cattle crush used for examination or vet treatment) and he was concerned that the vet's small frame put her at risk of injury if Boonmee shifted suddenly with the discomfort of the procedure.

"I said 'I will do it'. I know now that it was stupid, because with a three or 4000 kilo animal, it does not matter if you are 60kg or 90kg, you risk getting hurt either way," he says. "I went behind the elephant, and the mahout was in front, feeding her fruit in water to keep her occupied. Another one was standing on the rails so he could see what was going on and the back. I took the hose and with soap, I started doing what I had to do with her anus. I reached quite far in, about up to my shoulder, and I could feel the blockage and substance and slowly tried to move it out. She started to push back, and the guy on the rails did not see that because he was on his phone. The people in front were busy feeding her and could not see me because of her size.

"She pushed backwards, and then took one, two steps back and squeezed me into the thick metal poles that were behind me. I tried to call for help but there was no air in my lungs. I threw my other hand up but nobody saw it and after a time, I fell unconscious."

Edwin says his memory of fading out was seeing himself in a wooden white box at the local temple, his last thoughts that it was where he would soon be. Later inspection of the CCTV footage revealed the entire incident took place over about seven minutes. When his staff realised he was in trouble, they enticed the elephant forward, and Edwin fell to the ground, and in doing so, his arm fell out of the elephant's bottom. Striking the ground roused him, and he says survival instinct kicked in enough to make him move away a little.

"My arm was out and of course she started pooing and pissing. I got it on me: the most dramatic golden shower ever," he says. "I guess I was a bit like a dog being hit by a car because I stood up and walked to my house. I really don't know how I did that, but I did."

When Noi came home after getting word of the incident, she found Edwin collapsed in the bathroom. He had two broken ribs, three bruised ribs and his spine between the fourth and fifth vertebrae was displaced. He was in excruciating pain for many months. Four days later, Edwin had to fly to The Netherlands for meetings. He was in such pain that he spent as much of the flight as possible standing up. For two months, he could not sleep any other way than on his belly after crawling commando-style onto the bed.

"For a few minutes, when I realised no one knew I was being crushed, I really thought it was the end. I am glad it wasn't, but I also realise it was caused by my stupidity, thinking I could do the job better than a vet because I was bigger and stronger. Against a huge animal like that, if she really wanted to kill you or get you out of her way, no human would stand a chance."

Boonmee died after a short illness in April 2019. She had enjoyed more than six years of freedom at WFFT.

10. Two Tribes

There is a saying that no good deed goes unpunished.

So it was with Edwin's intervention in a situation that was not his, but which he felt called for his involvement to right terrible, crushing wrongs. But he could not have known this would bring him to the brink of physical collapse and emotional exhaustion, and it very nearly spelt the end of his wildlife rescue organisation.

Between Christmas and New Year 2011, an informant tipped Edwin off that in a wooded, scrubby area near Pa La-u, where wild elephants lived, two female elephants had been found dead and bloating deep in the forest. A second tipster told him that there were three more dead elephants, this time close to a village, and they had been shot. Edwin set out to see for himself with the area's village chief, who was from the Karen people, an ethnic minority group that lives there.

"When I got to the elephants, I saw that two of them were complete, but had been shot in the temple and the side. What was particularly strange was that one of them had tusks, had ivory, and that remained, so I knew this slaughter was not done by ivory traders," Edwin says. "It was also strange that there were tracks of a car, and there were drag marks on the ground. I know what that means now, but the penny did not drop for me just then."

A couple of days later, a local newspaper article detailed elephants being killed for their tusks, their trunk and their genitals. It said that there was a black Honda CRV seen driving in and out overnight that had been linked to a wildlife restaurant in Phuket. The article claimed the parts of the elephant had been used for food, including the trunk being used for sashimi, which Edwin had never heard of before.

"I looked at the pictures published in other newspapers that showed the scene from different angles and realised they were the two elephants I saw. But I and some of the villagers had seen them complete."

Edwin went to the village chief, who told him that some people had been attacked by government officials and that the same officials had also burned down a small village in the forest to move the people away from there. The officials were clearly going hard in an attempt to clear the area of human observation. Edwin began to do his own investigations and became increasingly uncomfortable with the inconsistencies and holes in the story. He spoke to locals knowledgeable about the area, and then went to Rat Buri to talk to a contact in the illegal wildlife trade. Soon after came the piece of the puzzle that had been missing.

An informant told Edwin that two quite young baby elephants had been taken to the district of Suan Pheung in Rat Buri. Edwin travelled to the region and to his horror, observed an obviously stressed baby elephant there. Rocking, squeaking and straining, the baby was clearly suffering in its captivity; the signs were clear to Edwin that the calf was wild-born and very recently taken.

Over the past decades, illegal wildlife traders have developed a fairly consistent strategy to collect baby elephants. After luring a group close to the road over time with food, a baby elephant is surreptitiously darted near an access point. The calf eventually falls under the spell of the anaesthetic, and the nannies – the team of older females in any elephant group who always hover around and care for a baby – become agitated about the sudden silence and stillness in it.

The poachers then scare off the adults, sometimes using guns, but if the nannies won't leave the calf, they are shot, leaving them either fleeing and injured or dead on the spot. Either is acceptable to the poachers.

The unconscious baby is then dragged using a winch into an enclosed pickup truck that has been customised with bolstered suspension. In a typical operation, the five or six people required will split the fee for extracting an elephant calf from the wild. In 2012, the bounty was about 200,000 baht, which was enough to give each of them a good life for many months.

The poachers would then take the calf to a Karen village where there is an old-fashioned knowledge of elephant training.

The baby's spirit would be broken in a process similar to the Phajaan or elephant crushing. The charge for that process is somewhere around 50,000 baht. The infant is put through a torturous sequence of events involving being tied up, beaten, starved and made to feel fear at the hands of its captors. The procedure is deliberately hard and painful, stripping a baby of every comfort and security. And somewhere, eventually, in the midst of the unthinkably cruelty, the calf will let out a cry of a particular pitch and tenor. It might take a month or so because the elephant spirit is strong even in a baby, but this is the signal the captors wait for.

It means that the calf is effectively no longer wild because its spirit is broken, its malleable brain twisted and its sense of security ripped asunder. It means the baby is cowed and submissive to those whom it depends on for food. Then starts the next phase of the process. A new baby arriving in an elephant camp cannot go unnoticed, so an intermediary dealer is charged with teaming up a baby with an adult female. Desperate for care and affection after being separated from other elephants for so long, the calf recently removed so suddenly from its mother will seek any comfort and cling to any adult female. It will cry and crowd the female, grabbing on to any inkling of attention or affection. A cow elephant will instinctively look after a calf and they are kept together for as long as it takes for them to develop a bond. Then, when the time and opportunities are right, they will be sold to a camp where no one has known the mother. The traders will claim the pair came from a camp in Surin or an elephant park in Chang Mai or Pattaya. Everyone thinks they are a mother and baby and their behaviour does not betray that.

Eventually, to legitimise the life and pairing, the calf is registered.

In 2012 a baby elephant would fetch about 1.2 million baht. Today, they are worth more than two million baht. Females are particularly valuable. There was a loophole in 2012, that if an elephant calf was born in captivity, an owner had nine years to register it, allowing plenty of time for fraud.

Edwin felt sure he had stumbled on a textbook case of stealing a wild elephant and illegally trading it, and that officials had been on the take to enable it to occur. Incensed at the greed and fired by outrage at the case of the five dead elephants near

Pa La-u, he went to the National Parks authorities, telling them that he had it from very good sources that four or five of their officials were involved in the crime. Out of hand, they dismissed his report, saying the ways in which he had drawn the conclusion was illogical. He felt as if he had been slapped and the patronising way they disregarded his information offended him.

He fired up. Never one to let what he felt was an obvious injustice against wild animals go, Edwin made contact with a journalist he trusted at *The Nation* in Bangkok, Jim Pollard, who assured him this was in fact an important news story that was in the public interest. He wrote a comprehensive article and the story, headlined Thai Elephants Being Killed for Tourist Dollars, ran over half a page in *The Nation* on January 24, 2012.

Little did Edwin know that the publication would unleash hell.

Almost immediately, the National Parks authorities began sequential raids on elephant camps, reporting that all was in order and no wild elephants were working there.

"I knew this was absolutely untrue. I knew this was a well-organised crime group that worked in the Pa La-u area and around the border with Burma that had connections in the right places to be able to supply wild elephants to trekking camps. It was not a small operation, and the fact that the authorities found nothing wrong in the many camps around was incredulous," Edwin says.

Edwin knew that the authorities would come to check his operation at WFFT, given they had elephants there. He expected it, wanting the opportunity to have the animals and his paperwork vetted and his operation officially acknowledged as being clean and in order. But while the rhythm of checks seemed above board and predictable, suddenly Edwin sensed there was more at play than checking paperwork on elephants. Elephant Nature Park in Chang Mai was checked on February 8 and word filtered through that owner Lek Chailert's animals were impounded because she could not show documents for 18 of her elephants. Edwin felt the prickle of alarm, knowing that in one of the world's most corrupt systems, the rules changed and anything was possible. And he knew it was he who had unleashed this beast, and it was he who was likely to be made to suffer most.

At 10.30 am on February 13, about 150 heavily armed police, military, border patrol and National Parks officers and 40 members of media, driving in a convoy, arrived at the WFFT rescue centre in Khao Luk Chang. Three Hummers with large machine guns perched atop were stationed at the gates. Border police officers sealed the compound, being pushy and aggressive. The 50 or so volunteers there were alarmed and upset, worried about the animals they were caring for but also for themselves. Some of the police, soldiers and officials spat in the faces of the volunteers and others made degrading comments to the female volunteers and staff. The elephant checking operation featured a great deal of swagger and noise, and it seemed the over-the-top invasion and display of force was designed to unsettle and interfere with daily activities at the centre. Edwin felt sick with stress and had a creeping feeling of foreboding that catastrophe was looming.

"I said to Noi, 'this is not about checking our elephants. I can feel it. Something big is about to happen'," he says. "To say I was worried for our animals and our staff and volunteers is an understatement, but there was absolutely nothing I could do but wait to see what they had in store for me."

Edwin also had another worry; he had a day of overstay on his visa. He had plans to go to Europe the next day and instead of going through the process of getting a visa extension for those two days, he planned to pay for the overstay as he left the country, a practice not uncommon among foreigners in Thailand. He had done it before, but this would be the last time Edwin would stretch and test the boundaries on visa regulations.

Until 2 pm that first day, all communication with the officers was related to elephants. But then they asked that all the paperwork including the police reports linked to the collection of any animal and the registration papers of that animal, be supplied for all the 300 wild animals housed at on the centre grounds. Noi panicked because her filing system was not well organised and it was not easy to gain rapid access to all the requested hard-copy documents. They were given a deadline of two hours, after which no more paperwork would be accepted. To produce so many documents for so many animals in that timeframe was physically impossible. Edwin felt a familiar stirring of rage at the injustice and a portent of doom.

Staff scrambled to meet the request, but the deadline came and the paperwork had not been produced for 103 animals. Edwin was told those creatures would be taken into the government's possession.

"I spoke to the deputy director-general of the Department of National Parks on the phone in Bangkok – he was at a tiger meeting with some international visitors – and he said he would try to buy us time. But it was clear to me that even if he wanted to do something, he couldn't. His boss, the National Parks Department director-general Damrong Pidech was after me; I know that now. He wanted my blood because I had made claims of corruption and illegal wildlife trading by his officers. His high position meant that no one could intervene in defence of me. We were trapped and, they were going to bring down terrible, unfair things on us and our operation."

At 6 pm, the assembled officers said they were arresting Edwin as the head of the Foundation for illegally holding animals. But Edwin told them he was not the president of the Foundation board any more (there had been a recent shuffle of positions) so Noi, as president, was taken in his place. Noi says she felt moments of extreme fear.

"Certainly, I was frightened when I was taken by the police, but I think the worst part was when they took my fingerprints at the police station," she says. She spent a harrowing night in a holding cell before the Khao Luk Chang village chief Fai used his position to guarantee 200,000 baht for Noi's bail, and she was released. Noi says she still feels grateful to him every day for that. Edwin says he still felt hopeful that the authorities would back off and be simply happy that they had shaken him, Noi and the Foundation a little.

"I perhaps naively thought that when we went to court, we could produce the paperwork for the remaining animals and the case would be dissolved," Edwin says. "It made logical sense to me because I knew that we had done nothing wrong. Our operation, our purpose and our function was simply to look after rescued animals, and we do that very well. I felt sure they would see and honour that, that if we did not have these animals in our care, they would not be likely to be cared for at all or would have far worse lives. I thought they would see that all was in order.

"How wrong I was about that."

Edwin flew to Kuala Lumpur in February 14 to renew his visa, planning to return later that day. At 2 pm, Noi called, hysterical. The convoy of trucks had returned to the rescue centre, but this time the officers had cages. She screamed down the phone to him that the officials had begun stalking the grounds in pursuit of the rescued animals for whom paperwork had not been produced by the deadline. The animals were stressed, the volunteers were crying and yelling and the staff were screaming and scared. The calm place of safety for the rescued animals had been thrown into a whirlwind, and pandemonium had been unleashed.

"I told Noi to slow it down, to start with the most difficult animals to catch and to block the officials' way and struggle to find keys," Edwin says. "I told her, 'don't help. Don't point at anything. Just tell them I am on my way back.' I have few words for how terrible it was, how distressing it was for everyone."

Six animals were taken away on the afternoon of February 14. Among this first group were three civets, which are not protected under Thai law and were returned later.

When Edwin arrived home in the evening, the mayhem that had been visited upon them had settled in, literally. He found officers had taken up residence on the grounds. Tents were erected and hammocks were strung up. The officers were using the compound's toilets and shouting abuse at the volunteers. The gates were locked, and Edwin and Noi were forbidden from taking items in or out of their home, which is at the centre of the grounds. The employees' business activities and daily routines were observed, their movements watched. The mood was menacing and hostile.

In every way possible, the wildlife rescue centre was under siege. And worse was to come.

"They hired private people to catch the animals and some were hunters; you can imagine how horrible that was for us," Edwin says. "Some of the drug users who live behind our lake were also hired by the government to catch the animals. The animals, these animals who had already suffered abuse at the hands of humans and to whom we had promised safety and a good life, were being chased down and struck. It was disgusting and distressing, but I knew that I must play it cool. I knew I had to stay in control, and I thought that I couldn't stop it, but I could fight back using social media and with formal applications to put an end to this unfair attack."

The colonel of the army who was in command of the soldiers ordered to help the National Parks officers take the animals approached Edwin on February 16, saying he felt there was something wrong. He remarked on the beauty of the grounds, the openness of the animal enclosures and how healthy the animals were. Edwin says the colonel made some phone calls and then indicated someone from the highest ranks would be in touch. He then stated he would not be part of the raid and took all his soldiers away, never to return. The military involvement in the operation was over.

But the collection of animals by others seconded to do the harrowing task continued.

In the meantime, Edwin's Facebook posts garnered the eyes of the virtual world, and media and public attention had been piqued. On February 17, journalists began to swarm as support for Edwin and the centre grew. The injustice and the animals' stories struck a chord with a compassionate public.

Then acclaimed Thai singer Tom Dundee swept in on his Harley Davidson and stood between the animals and the police, saying they would have to arrest him before removing any more animals. He said Thailand should be happy and proud to have a place where its persecuted animals were treated so well. The media lapped it up.

Suddenly on Friday, February 17, at 3 pm, perhaps in response to the focus that only a celebrity can create, the law enforcement officers and contracted animal catchers suddenly cleared off. By then they had been limited by the obstruction of the volunteers and chaos of so many people being around to taking about 20 animals. Social media attention magnified, with Facebook and Instagram users worldwide posting short clips of support, saying they were with WFFT and calling for the animals to be freed. Footage of the authorities hitting a baby monkey with sticks in its enclosure and knocking it into a tub of water went viral.

Edwin had approaches from international media including Voice of America, BBC and National Geographic – all wanting to cover the story. But while animal lovers were outraged, the shadows of power began to cast a pall over the events. The coverage of the raids and the threatened criminal charges led to sponsors withdrawing support. The stress was starting to show. Edwin, always a strongly built man, lost 5kg in a week. He was to lose three more before the confiscations stopped. Sleep was fragmented and disturbed. His mind raced and his fears that the life he had built for the rescued animals was about to be ripped apart took root in the pit of his stomach.

On February 21, Edwin was told the National Parks Department director Damrong Pidech was concerned about the attention the raid was getting and was coming to see its operation for himself. About 100 media representatives were in tow.

In front of rolling cameras, the National Parks boss formally told Edwin he was going to file charges over the Foundation's trespass on forest land and said WFFT was cutting down trees without permission. He told the media the Foundation was running a hospital without a licence. He threatened to arrest the abbot of the local temple for taking 40,000 baht a month in rent for property he did not own (this was incorrect; the temple received a peppercorn rent of 1200 baht a month from the Foundation). Damrong said he was going to have all of the centre's animals removed, not just those for which paperwork had not been produced and have the centre shut down. He told the assembled media the centre received millions in government funding and all of it went into the pockets of Edwin and Noi, who lived a lavish life.

Every point was untrue, but he would not back down nor let Edwin rebut his claims in front of the media, and he left in a showy flurry via a helicopter that landed at the nearby temple grounds. The reputational harm created was catastrophic.

On February 22, a dozen veterinarians arrived with cages to aid the removal of the remaining animals. Volunteers conducted sit-ins at enclosure entrances to block access; staff locked cages and threw away keys. But there was no stopping the cleanout.

Emotionally shredded and feeling helpless, Edwin reverted to a behavioural habit: he deliberately switched gears. The physical removal continued, but he began to consider his legally available defences. In every way, the seizures were in response to violations of unwritten procedures, not breaches of the law. But despite WFFT having correct paperwork for all but three leopard cats that had come in in the days before the raid that had not had time to be processed yet, no further documents would be accepted.

Then a lifeline was seemingly thrown.

Popular afternoon news show on Channel 3, Sorrayuth, contacted Edwin, saying they wanted to have a live on-air interview with him and Damrong for the lead-in to the 6 pm news. The producer initially gave Edwin one time, then called back indicating he wanted Edwin to come into the station later. During the three-hour drive from the rescue centre to Bangkok, Edwin was told by contacts that Damrong was already on air, making claims Edwin had a criminal record in Holland, had fled the Dutch military without leave, was stealing the wildlife of Thailand for his own gain and was, in general, a despicable character. Edwin contacted the station, asking for an explanation, to be told that Damrong's authority and the existence of pending charges against Edwin meant that he had to be given the uninterrupted chance to explain the department's position before Edwin was to come on air. Edwin said he felt this was unfair but would still come on the program.

"I had a business card from a reporter/producer at Channel 5, the military channel, and I thought to myself about how the military had been relatively positive to me during the raid," Edwin says. "I called the guy at Channel 5, who said he was watching Channel 3 with interest.

"I asked if I could get on Channel 5 exactly after the Royal Anthem at 6 pm and give my side of the story. I said if he could arrange it, I would be there with my wife and the documentation. I also told him I would bring over all the viewers from Channel 3.

"I called Channel 3 and told them I was stuck in traffic, and then I drove to Channel 5. I was in the makeup chair when I called Channel 3 and told them I could not make it and needed to do the interview by telephone.

"The anchor assured me I was live when I said 'I could not make it to your studio because what you are doing to me is not fair, and I hate unfairness and injustice more than anything. You have allowed Damrong Pidech to stitch me up and defame my name and my Foundation and not given me a real chance to defend myself. Watch Channel 5 at 6 pm.' and I hung up."

Edwin says there was some satisfaction in taking back some control of a terrible situation and in having his voice heard.

On Channel 5, the anchor did not let him off the hook. She asked several tough questions but allowed him to answer. By the end of the show, bolstered by positive feedback on the ticker tape at the bottom of the screen, Edwin felt the tide of opinion against him was on the turn.

On February 24, the last animal was removed from the WFFT wildlife rescue centre. The social media campaign was ramped up, and Edwin lobbied politicians, requesting a parliamentary committee to look into the conduct of those involved in the raid and the motivation behind it. They agreed and ruled the raid was unnecessary but could not comment on the legality of a case before the courts.

In October 2012, Edwin, Noi and the Foundation were officially charged with illegal possession of wildlife and running an animal hospital without the correct permit. Eventually, the hospital documentation charges were dropped against Edwin and the Foundation, but Noi (as president) was ultimately fined 5000 baht, even though WFFT had lodged an application for the hospital registration before the raid.

The raid and the fallout made international news, with the big networks such as CNN, the BBC and ABC all covering it in detail. The results were both good and bad, with wildlife advocates and everyday people rallying behind WFFT, but some sponsors and commentators backing away.

In May 2013, four government officials were found guilty in relation to the poaching of the elephants in the park near Pa La-u. They were each fined 20,000 baht and given a suspended jail term because it was their first offences.

Edwin, Noi and the Foundation were issued with 30,000 baht fines and eight-month suspended jail terms for illegally keeping wildlife. They appealed and on February 28, 2014, their convictions and sentences were overturned. The prosecutor appealed against their exonerations to the highest court.

But Edwin continued to hold his head high. He attended the 2013 CITES conference when it was held in Bangkok, staffing a booth showing WFFT's work.

"I was known because of the raid and in some ways that was both uncomfortable professionally and a difficulty for me personally," Edwin says. "There were important organisations from America, Africa and Europe there and delegates knew me, and I knew why. Some of the Thai government officials are looking at me, thinking 'what is this asshole doing here? He is a criminal to us', even though the final court decision had not been made. There were also people who were ashamed of what had happened to me; charging someone with a high profile who rescues wildlife with illegal wildlife possession is preposterous to the rest of the world.

"I was showing strength, though. I was dressed for the occasion and held my head up. I shook hands and said hello to people. I also made a bit of fun too, in the middle of it all, because I always do that. This was my payback, my way of saying I am still here, and I am still in charge. I also made a big presentation about the illegal trade in orang-utans and made it very plain that this was a huge operation, and I knew all about it."

Opposite WFFT's CITES stand was a booth run by Wild Animal Rescue, the organisation that Edwin had joined in his first tentative steps into a life dedicated to rescuing animals. The proximity gave him pause for thought; he had chosen to go his own way, create his own kind of rescue centre that delivered animals as close to a wild life as he could. The approach was revolutionary, and the price paid had been high because that meant riling authorities and existing operations.

But despite the shadows still hanging over him, Edwin felt deep within that to do it any other way would not have been authentic to himself. The arm of the law proved to be long indeed. Months morph into years sometimes, but whispers for justice can still become a call.

Edwin, Noi and the Foundation had final absolution when an appeal against the overturning of their convictions and sentences, lodged by prosecutors, was dismissed by the Supreme Court on January 31, 2017.

They may have been cleared, but the scars and the memory of the pain remain.

Life's lessons and experiences have a way of reverberating in those like Edwin, who live deliberately.

11. Eye of the Tiger

It is widely believed that trafficking in wildlife – whether in parts or whole, dead or alive – is the second most lucrative illicit business on the planet, taking a sinister position above weapons but below drugs.

Asia's nations have a plethora of bionetworks and therefore boast an extraordinary array of wildlife species. Creatures in great numbers are being illegally caught, trapped or hunted all over Thailand; on all the islands of Indonesia, including Sumatra and Borneo, and on mainland Malaysia. The pathways over land and sea are well worn, with long and winding routes funnelling neatly into markets all over Asia, but in particular Vietnam and China. Those two nations take the lead in sharing massive human populations and having an insatiable hunger and thirst for wildlife, driven by outdated traditional beliefs and a desire for anything special or exotic. In October 2018, China stunned the world by reversing a 25-year official ban on using tiger parts and rhinoceros horn for scientific and medical purposes.

Thailand and Laos are acknowledged as the biggest transit point of illegal wildlife for the Chinese market. This eclectic, lucrative business includes everything from tigers and bears to snakes and pangolin. And if it flies, walks or swims, someone in China will eat it or use it for medication. That is the core of the problem.

In Thailand, if a person trades across borders in illicit drugs such as methamphetamines or heroin, there is a risk they will be put to death for their crime and their family can lose everything. But if caught trafficking in illegal wildlife, they risk a maximum of $US1200 fine and perhaps a year in jail, with the prison term likely to be suspended. The profits made from the illicit drugs and wildlife trades are thought to be comparable, which makes wildlife trafficking appealing to criminal groups.

An adult tiger bought from a tiger farm – and there are more than 30 operating in Thailand under various guises – might cost about 150-200,000 baht. When it crosses the Thai-Laos border, its value is about 100,000 baht more, and when it finally reaches the Laos-China border, the same animal is delivered for between 500-700,000 baht: within a thousand kilometres, a tiger's value triples. This is an example of the profitable, cold-hearted business Edwin has pledged to disrupt. But to do this effectively, he must also dip his own toes into the sordid, grimy waters.

"When you are a butcher, you have to deal with the blood; it gets on your clothes and on your hands. When you work with elephants, you get shit on your hands, and if you are a mechanic, you get marked by oil and grease. Because I am concerned with the illegal wildlife trade, I have to get the blood, shit, and grease on me," he says. "I would be foolish to think I could do anything by simply standing back and analysing the traders and their activities. The only way to really know is to hear about it from them and to see it for myself."

Edwin's involvement as a disruptor of illegal wildlife transactions began not long after the genesis of his rescue work almost two decades ago. Never one to skate on the surface of an issue or keep quiet when he sees something that riles him, he soon realised the individual animals coming into his care were the living, breathing by-products of a bountiful industry that had learnt to move nimbly in the shadows.

Perhaps ironically, the best information Edwin gets about illicit wildlife activities and shipments comes from the traders themselves. As with any competitors in a lawless market, the dealers are very keen to rip each other off and to shut each other down, and sometimes that means Edwin must do deals with an enemy. He has been compelled to pay for information on occasion, but he has gained a reputation among his contacts for being reliable, and this is not often needed. He has four long-term, well-placed contacts in the illegal wildlife trade whom he talks to at least once a month, plus many other bit-players in the supply chain.

"It is vital for me that I keep some of those relationships going, so I must also give information occasionally in return," he says. "It is also important to the continuation of my work in this area that my most valued contacts are protected when they give me information. It cannot be traced back to them and that is for my own self-interest, not their preservation. I therefore have to be very careful about who I share information with and how I give it."

Edwin is often criticised for his contact with wildlife traffickers, but says this is how investigators and law enforcers the world over operate, and he has simply adapted that approach to suit himself. Any relationship between two groups involves give and take, or it breaks down.

Edwin is now very well connected with trusted friends in high places, but has been burnt in a minor way before, in the years when he did not realise how extensive the corruption could be within Thai officialdom. He once made the mistake of passing on information that was used to accelerate rather than shut down an operation, and line an official's already-fat pockets in the backdraft. His caution is also fostered by the chance of very real consequences: over the past 20 years at least 13 environmental activists interfering in the illegal wildlife trade have died under suspicious circumstances in Thailand.

"I can't give the police all the information I have because the corrupt ones – and there are many – would take that information to the illegal wildlife traders and say 'I know this about you and you need to pay me more money not to arrest you'. That is how it sometimes works in Southeast Asia. I accept that, so I do not share information often or until I am sure, and then if I do it is only with certain high-ranking police officers," Edwin says. "For small things, I can't go to them. Those organisations that provide all information to the police are actually just adding more money to corrupt police's pockets. You must be very careful if your intention is really to help the animals and not just achieve some legal involvement."

There is more than a modicum of patience needed, as with any disruption of business dealings that profit from illegality. Nerves of steel are required as well, and relying on energy generated by head, not heart. Edwin can be hot-headed, but he says when an occasion requires it, he focuses on the greater good.

"For example, I know about a group of people shipping tigers from Thailand into Laos at the moment. But I cannot reveal that information to the police without endangering my source. For now, I have to let it go," he says. "While it is upsetting that this is going on right now, in the long term, if we play it well, by the end of the year I will be able to share the information and make a major kill and take down a whole group, not just one or two individuals. There are victims now, yes: tigers are being moved and killed. But you have to weigh up the costs and benefits and not get weighed down in the meantime."

Edwin says he could tip off the authorities about a group of say four or five people who might ship 50 to 100 tigers a year, but even if they are taken into custody, within 48 hours a family member or friend will stand up and take it over, akin to cutting off a snake's head and two more popping up in its place.

"But if we can get the whole network at once, the business model is gutted and there is nothing to trade," he says. "That means hunters, providers, farmers, drivers, and those who form the market in China and Laos. It is the only way to really knock it down. It basically halves the trade in one go. That is the ideal, and that is very difficult to achieve.

"Any organisation that claims they know how many micro operators there are in the illegal trade of wildlife is bullshitting. The big NGOs like WWF like to come out with these reports that they have done research on this, and they put numbers on it, but I know they don't speak to the illegal wildlife traders because hardly any of them speak the bloody language," he says. "Nobody knows if they have caught 10 per cent of the illegal trade, when it could be just one per cent. The numbers are designed to show they have good results, which then can be turned into proper tools for fundraising. I am not saying they are not making a difference, but this is the tip of the iceberg. Things are getting worse; no matter how much positive information is being shared."

The illegal trade of tigers, bears and pangolin is big money. Pangolin, which are solitary and known as 'the belt animal' in some nations, are scratched from the wild one at a time. They have a diet of a particular species of ant, but the poachers force-feed them a mix including flour and water so that they weigh more. When the purchase price is by the kilo, cruelty and pain do not hold much weight. They also must be moved quickly, as it is hard-to-impossible to breed them in captivity, unlike tigers and bears.

Edwin says there are only one or two big operators in the tiger trade that move animals between Thailand, Laos and China, but there are many single operators who deal with one or two tigers at a time. He would not dare to put a number on these. It is estimated there are about 1700 tigers in Thailand, of which only 200 are wild. That leaves 1500 being exploited in the tourism industry and kept in tiny cages at tiger farms.

They are aptly lauded as magnificent, lithe, apex predators, but those properties also make them highly desirable, with an assumption that the consumption of the tiger's body parts can transfer that ferocity, strength and beauty. China is the biggest consumer of tiger parts in the world, with Vietnam also being a massive market. There are farms in Thailand and a smaller number in Laos, and together, Thailand and Laos also provide the geographical channel for the flow to China and Vietnam. Although Thailand has recently made noises about clamping down on the illegal trade in tigers, Laos authorities are not acting on enforcing the laws. Tiger farm numbers there are growing, even though they promised in September 2016 during the CITES conference in South Africa to close down all tiger farms in the country.

Regardless of education and awareness of tigers' preciousness and vulnerability as a species in the West, the appetite in some Asian markets continues unabated. Tigers are wanted for their striking skin, but even more for their bones, teeth and penises. Importantly, some governments including China do not see problems that originate beyond their borders as their own; they are simply consumers of the products of someone else's issues. Thus, the cycle is allowed to endlessly roll.

"The government says there are no tiger farms, but if a facility has only one kind of animal, it is a farm," Edwin says. "They breed them, exploit them at a young age after being taken away from their mothers, fatten them once they have no tourism value, and then they disappear. Officially, they do not kill them, but we see numerous babies continuously in these farms and you do not need a PhD to work out what is going on when you do not see the older tigers in the same numbers."

Most farms pose as small tourist attractions where people can go and pat a tiger. The biggest of these was, of course, the first version of the Tiger Temple.

The Tiger Temple started in 1999. There was an elephant camp in the Sai Yok district of Kanchanaburi province that had two tiger cubs chained up for photo opportunities for the tourists who came to ride the elephants. The camp owners did not have a zoo licence for those cubs; it simply owned the elephants. It was against the law, and they felt the looming heat of officialdom and the rapidly-growing needs of the tigers, so wanted to offload them.

"They put the tigers up for sale," Edwin says. "The abbot at the temple at Kanchanaburi, which was a big temple then but nothing like the size it is now, thought to himself that he has two gibbons on chains in his temple already; he had some deer and some other animals walking around. How great would it be to get a few tigers! Monks and tigers: now that could be interesting.

"So he bought the tigers. He paid 100,000 baht per tiger – at the time, quite a lot of money. Some say it was 100,000 for both but I heard from the traders who were involved that it was 100,000 each."

The cubs were young and playful. Tourists were entranced by their fun and enchanted by their play and posted a couple of videos on YouTube, including one of a young gibbon on a chain swinging down and bopping the cub on the head and going back into the tree. Suddenly people far and wide wanted to see these creatures for themselves. Monks with tigers had appeal to Thai people on a religious level and little groups of tourists came in on the way to the Sai Yok Noi waterfall to get photos with them. Pretty soon the chief monk became a bit of a celebrity, claiming he was the inventor of 'conservation, Asian-style'.

"He bought two more tigers, this time from a crocodile farm in Rat Buri province owned by someone who was at that time a Member of Parliament, a man I will call Mr C. It turns out that the first two tigers also originally came from Mr C, but that was not found out until later."

With four tigers at the temple, Edwin decided to go and have a look for himself. By then he had a tiger too; the big cat he had rescued from the gas station, Meow.

"I was curious because I was pretty new at this, and I thought I could learn something about how they were kept. But I found he kept them on a chain during the day and at night in the house, nothing special really. I was not impressed but not really alarmed by it even though I knew he did not have the correct licensing."

The temple's popularity with tourists blossomed, and the abbot started to breed the tigers. There were three offspring, so that made seven tigers by 2002. That was the first time he was raided by the then-Forestry Department, but was allowed to keep the tigers.

"There were a lot of people going to see the tigers, and the local officials wanted them to be kept there because it brought tourists," Edwin says. "Basically the director-general allowed him to keep the tigers because the Forestry Department did not have the facilities to keep the tigers then. They had some rescue centres, but they were not equipped to house and care for tigers. The budget was not big and tigers are expensive." The abbot was charged and officials started court action but the case was dropped soon afterwards.

"The abbot must have felt invincible," Edwin says. "He began to accelerate the breeding and buying. By 2007-08, he had 60 or 70 tigers. The business became bigger. He charged 500 baht to enter the temple and 1200 baht to get a photograph. He charged 6000 baht for a morning with the cubs.

"The babies were taken from their mothers straight away so that the tourists could feed them milk. This is a familiar setup, used by keepers of attractive wildlife around the world. With lions in Africa, they do the same thing for the canned hunting market there.

"The abbot became wealthy and powerful for a while. He started to exchange tigers with other facilities and also abroad, which is against the Convention on International Trade in Endangered Species of Wild Fauna and Flora treaty. We found evidence of that in 2009 – other people did as well – and brought it to the attention of the authorities but nothing was done for more than seven more years."

Just before its downfall, the Tiger Temple was believed to have raked in 330,000 baht a day. The abbot exchanged tigers with a Laos farm to diversify the breeding pool. He exchanged lions for tigers, and he bought hornbills, bears and all kinds of other protected animals.

"He claims he rescued them but no one is going to give you a healthy tiger for free," Edwin says. "No one is going to give you a couple of highly endangered hornbills, especially not in combination of male and female. An illegal trafficker from Bangkok told me that that particular species had been ordered, not just delivered. That is not rescue: that is trade."

In 2015, the head monk applied for a zoo licence. He had set up a company called Tiger Temple Company Limited, which bought a piece of land next to the temple, and he applied for a zoo permit for it. The government had no option but to approve the application and the trade became more open. Media outlets began to run stories on tiger disappearances and fluctuating numbers of the big cats at the temple. The authorities came under pressure.

"I then made a complaint to the administrative court in Bangkok, saying that when the authorities claimed they had evidence against me, they did everything to go after me," Edwin says. "Then why is no one going after the Tiger Temple? I argued it was selective enforcement."

The administrative court did not want to take the case, but it did put some pressure on the DNP, and there were people there who told Edwin they were quite pleased with what he had done. A DNP official called Edwin and asked if he was going to sue them. Edwin said he was not, but that they must investigate the by-now very large number of complaints and concerns about the tigers at the temple.

"I said that if they did not follow up, that would be being derelict in their duty; that is the legal status. They are compelled by law to follow up a legitimate complaint. But this is a military government, and you have to play it carefully, and it does not always follow the expected path," he says.

Edwin had come by extensive information about the connection between the Tiger Temple and the use of traffickers through Laos and within Thailand. He had contacts among officials there who confirmed everything they had suspected, and far, far more.

Edwin and his WFFT team orchestrated social media campaigns, which took off.

Early in 2016, the Thailand Government's Department of National Parks acted. The raid attracted some media attention. They vowed to take the tigers out five at a time. They had to scramble and build cages to accommodate them, but after taking the first group of tigers, the temple refused to co-operate and the abbot produced his renewed zoo permit for the land bordering the temple. The DNP had initially stated that they had planned to take out about 75 animals.

"We were really surprised that the DNP stopped. I thought they had more courage than that," Edwin says. "So I contacted them and pointed out there were more than a dozen hornbills in captivity, as well as jackals and bears. There were no licences for them. The government claimed not to have seen them and went in and began confiscating them. The abbot finally agreed to give up half the tigers, but then he did not follow through."

Under increased pressure, in May 2016, the authorities went in full throttle. The international media went into overdrive. Those who had visited with temple to get a photo realised the savagery they had helped to fund. The Thai Government was shamed and conservationists discovered a whole extra level of concern for the tiger population. There were a total of 147 tigers found alive at the temple and dozens more in freezers.

"Feeding and caring for them is a massive job and the DNP could not take that on all at once," Edwin says. "No one could; I do not blame them for that. It was a lot of money to build cages and look after them properly. This is not what we wanted, and not what the DNP wanted. We wanted them to be shared among facilities like ours."

But the abbot was fighting back as a mad dog and gave the DNP no choice but to clear the place out.

"I think the reports of killing the tigers for their parts and killing cubs for the market were incorrect," Edwin says. "I think they were stillborn cubs, which is not uncommon. It is common for tigers to die in the first few weeks after birth, especially in the circumstances in which they were kept. I don't think there was barbarism in that way at the temple. However, for all the amulets and pendants made of tiger parts, there was of course evidence of trade and ill-intent."

If a tiger dies, their body is still considered useful in Asia. The skin can be used and their bones harvested. Edwin suggests the skin and bones found in the raid were taken from those that died of sickness or old age.

"You have to understand the place of animals in Asian culture," he says. "For these people, it was business and for them a dead animal is an animal without feelings so they can do whatever they like with it. I don't agree, but I can see why they might have done that, given the culture.

"But for them to exploit an animal day-by-day for tourism and money is a complete different issue; it is barbaric, and it is disgusting. Taking a baby away from its mother days after being born purely for the tourist trade while still claiming you are conserving the species is an utter lie."

To date, no one has been charged as a result of the Tiger Temple raid. Charges are important, as under Thai law and regulation, a zoo permit can be blocked or revoked if any of the shareholders is convicted of illegal wildlife trading. The abbot is still at the temple, and those involved are still running their business, a set-up Edwin calls Tiger Temple 2.0, registered in the name of Tiger Temple Company Ltd. On paper, the temple and business are separate and from a legal point of view there was no reason to revoke their zoo permit.

The seized tigers remain at the government facilities, and many have died.

Thailand is one of 183 nations that are signatories to the 14th Convention on International Trade in Endangered Species agreement from 2007, which states that the keeping of tigers in captivity for commercial gain or breeding should be limited to conservation needs.

"But if they stop the Tiger Temple from keeping tigers, you have to stop the others too, and that is not going to be easy," Edwin says. "You cannot say this is conservation because you are not releasing these animals back in to the wild. Also, you are not conserving a species strictly native to Thailand because these are hybrid, interbred, tigers."

The Tiger Temple was granted a zoo permit in early 2016. A permit to move two dozen tigers from a now-defunct tiger farm in eastern Thailand is under consideration by authorities and is likely to be issued. The approval of the application will see the rebirth of Tiger Temple, or Tiger Zoo, or Golden Tiger as it might be called. The temple has also indicated it is looking at buying dozens more animals. Authorities initially slowed these requests down as it was deemed the 3 ha on which the new facility is built wouldn't provide enough space for such numbers.

Edwin says Tiger Zoo sets a precedent for other businesses, because it is tacit approval for what has been shown to be exploitation of wildlife, and it is fuelling the illegal wildlife trade, blurring the wafer thin line between legitimately making money from wildlife and the illegal wildlife trade, or what wildlife conservationists call the grey market. A tiger from a farm might be 200,000 baht, but one extracted from the wild is initially a lot cheaper because its cost is one man with one bullet.

"The ones from places like the temple are basically not wild animals because they are born in captivity. They are basically farm animals, and they are sold as such across borders," Edwin says. "Suddenly, because this has been allowed to go on, we have animals that should be wild, but are not. You get this grey space between what is legal and what is not legal, and you get traders and officials who hide in that grey zone. It sickens me; people seem to forget that when you have this trade in tigers, you are faced with opportunistic people. The money is just too good."

Edwin says tests have shown that about 10 per cent of the tigers detected in the illegal wildlife trade are not from farms, but are from the wild, despite protests to the contrary. In addition to Thailand's 200 wild tigers, Laos has perhaps one or two. Cambodia and Vietnam have none, and India and Bangladesh also have relatively meagre populations. Authoritative figures put the worldwide wild tiger population at about 4000. But that elite number pushes up their value, and the Chinese market is growing with its increasing wealth but rigid adherence to traditional tastes. At the same time, China is a signatory to the CITES agreement.

In Laos, also a signatory, there are about 700 tigers on farms. Edwin has seen the majority of them for himself. A few years ago, he observed three farms that also have bears close to the Thai-Laos border using a drone launched from Thailand side. The armed guards and high security indicated a valuable commodity was within. The shots they fired indicated they were prepared to fight for it.

"Thailand and Laos are gateways in the tiger trade. Thailand because of its fabulous infrastructure and Laos because it is a long strip of a country that has a long border with China. And in Laos, corruption is rife so that makes it perfect to push the animals through," Edwin says.

There have been several amnesties on kept wildlife in Thailand. The first had its genesis in the late 1980s. Under pressure when it became evident Thailand was a major player in international illegal trade in flora and fauna, the nation was threatened by CITES with a global trade ban unless it took steps to rein it in. The nation had no laws to protect its diverse wildlife or ecosystems, and they were forced into action.

In 1992, the country's first wildlife preservation legislation was enacted and with it came an amnesty. But it seemed old habits die hard, and the now-illegal trade in animals continued to flourish. Again, under threat by international sanctions, in 2003 the government introduced another 90-day amnesty to those keeping wildlife illegally ahead of a promised clean-out and crack down.

More than 1.1 million animals, including birds and reptiles that were from protected species, were registered. Bizarrely, it has been revealed that some people registered animals that they did not have but planned to acquire and wanted legally certainty. In that amnesty, Edwin registered 84 rescued animals that the authorities already knew he had. No one ever checked that those animals existed.

It is expected that when the current wildlife laws under development in Thailand are fully implemented and bedded down, another amnesty for some endangered species will be offered. Edwin expects there will be a flood of 400,000-500,000 registrations of international animals that are on the list of CITES as being banned from trade.

But knowing as he does the dark side of wildlife trade and treatment in Thailand, he fears it could be far more.

12. Take Me Home

Despite waves of loss, the anguish and the hardship, Edwin's desire to take rescued animals out of the hands of humans and deliver them into as wild a life as possible is insatiable. It is a hunger, a drive, a force that he himself cannot fully explain.

He says if he were a religious man – and he absolutely is not – the force within him might be a calling. With it comes elements of that which is thrust upon a person, and there have been dark times when he wished he could shake the responsibility and relentlessness of the work when the physicality of a rescue or the complexity of meeting the nebulous needs of an erratic procedural and legislative system are so massive they push over the edge of what is manageable.

But even when pushed to the doorway of exhaustion or madness, Edwin says he continues with the work because it not only needs to be done, but also because he feels he is the one who must do it. His creation is a voracious beast, indeed and the number of wild animals in need continues to grow.

There is an avalanche of support for his work. On the ground level, WFFT volunteers often come more than once, so challenging and enriching is the experience they have. And the practises and standards at the rescue centre and hospital are lauded in animal welfare and conservation circles as setting the standard for Asia. Edwin's advice on animal care protocols has been sought by authorities from far and wide.

But he says the waves of criticism roll in too, and he expects that never to abate. In personal communications, Edwin's brash directness can be confronting. Those who work close to him need a thick skin and self-confidence enough to deal with his sometimes-chiding comments and criticisms. At times, he appears to have little filter between his churning brain and mobile mouth.

"I can be an arsehole. And yes, I can be rude. I know that," he says. "But why would I change when it has helped me have the success I have? Without that, I am not sure I would have been able to achieve all I have for the animals. And anyway, if you climb a high tree, you catch a lot more wind."

Criticism about the accommodation of the rescued animals is harder to take. The centre has developed and expanded dramatically in the past 10 years in particular, and the enclosures now are far superior to those constructed in 2001. Edwin is proud of that.

"Things can be better, still: of course they can. That is still a drive for me," he says. "We are limited by funds and space, but I am also very proud of what we do and the conditions our rescued wildlife live in. If those who say that a cage or enclosure is too small could see where that animal came from, where we saved it from, they would see that in one moment, their living environment improved 300 per cent. You can't compare the two when you do not know.

"Some who come here are surprised that our animals are in enclosures. I don't know what they expect, some kind of fantasyland where predators and prey somehow lie down together? They must know little about animals if that is their idea of us."

Tommy, who is the chief of the elephant and wildlife rescue parts of the operation, says the constant review and updating of enclosures sat well with him as a conservationist and animal rescuer.

"I feel comfortable that almost all the time, we provide a far better environment than they have come from. That is satisfying," he says. "We have animals in quarantine in smallish spaces, but for example we have Gold, a macaque rescued from a temple, currently there in a cage that is 24 cubic metres or so.

"He lived in a cage outside that temple which was less than half a cubic metre for five years. He could not stretch out and was in his own waste. I rescued him myself. He doesn't know anything other than that cage and the one he is in now. Space and conditions are, as with all things, relative."

At the WFFT wildlife rescue centre, the animals that are in cages are kept in precincts so that they see others of their own species. Ideally, if they are ready (some come to the centre never having seen another of their own kind), they are housed in pairs and threes. Eventually, the monkeys will live in troupes, the bears in sleuths, the otters in bevies. Those that can be released into the wild will be freed in groups too. Those that have been captive for the longest are the most damaged. Some have been taught to pose, to please or to imitate human expression and stance. Many have been fed a human diet, including many on poor-nutrient junk food. The kindest approach is taken, and they are weaned off human interaction a little at a time.

"If you compare wild elephants to those here, of course ours do not have endless space. But our elephants have not had that in their whole adult lives," Edwin says. "They have not known that. But now they are here, they do not want for anything; they have stimulation, and they are unshackled and calm."

Animals are also not tormented by that exclusively human emotion, envy. They live day to day and have security where they are, regardless of human opinion of the size or quality of their space, or the size of their neighbour's space.

"People here say, 'you have an eco-lodge with people staying next to elephants. That is exploitation.' No, it isn't. It is giving people the chance to see elephants roaming and bathing and interacting with each other. The elephants get a choice. The enclosures are so large that if they do not want to be near people, they can walk away from them and out of sight. It is part of running a foundation sustainably, and ultimately, it is respecting the animals. It is all for the animals."

On occasion, Edwin has become involved in animal rescues, rehabilitation and repatriation missions that reach far beyond the WFFT rescue centre's geographical footprint.

Edwin has successfully organised the repatriation of 69 orang-utans to Indonesia from the various nations from which they were held captive. No single person or entity has ever repatriated that number of great apes. He was directly involved in agitating for the seizure of these beautiful animals once he became aware they were being held illegally. What sounds simple and right was a messy, grubby process.

Soon after Edwin had begun WFFT in 2001, he started to hear reports about an illegal trade in orang-utans. He says from the start, he was clear that he wanted to rescue and care for wild animals until they could be released, but at the time he had never had any notions of being engaged in investigating illegal wildlife trade and ultimately disrupting it. On reflection, he says that was possibly naïve, given his inquisitive, investigative nature, military background, strong sense of justice and the history and links of many of the animals that came into his care.

In 2002, Edwin heard from an illegal wildlife trader from near Bangkok that orang-utans were being trafficked in via an Indonesian boat company that had small and medium coastal vessels bringing in meat and vegetables and other merchandise from Indonesia, Malaysia and Singapore. The vessels docked at Sumut Sakhon, southwest of Bangkok.

Soon after, Edwin went to a market near the harbour and got talking to the woman at a noodle shop who had been there for many years, and whose husband worked on the docks. He asked if she had ever seen any monkeys coming off the boats or being held on the docks.

"She said, 'no, no monkeys – only apes'. That really surprised me because Thai people don't usually see the difference between an ape and a monkey. And then she said they were red ones, and used the word 'orang-utans'. That was special, and I knew my information was accurate. I could immediately feel the prickle of something big about to happen."

Edwin says the woman told him that every now and again, a vessel would dock, and some orang-utans would be unloaded, and sometimes the babies would just be carried ashore as a baby would, astride a human hip. Edwin formulated a plan. He sought more information from contacts about boat arrivals and on a subsequent visit saw with his own eyes orang-utans being unloaded from a boat in cobbled-together boxes made with two vegetable crates tied together.

Edwin and a Thai friend attached a magnetised GPS tracker to the underside of the bumper of the waiting Nissan Big M pick-up truck. It would emit a signal for three days, maximum, every 15 or 20 minutes. Edwin's friend gave him the map of where the vehicle had gone, and it became clear that it had been to a safari park in Bangkok several times and was parked at a house nearby at night. This enabled them to retrieve the tracker, but also provide evidence enough to Edwin that the destination of the orang-utans taken from the Indonesian boat was Safari World.

He had heard about cockatoos being illegally going to the same park, but this concerned him far more, and he had the evidence. That such a thing could be happening systematically to these beautiful, highly intelligent apes made him feel sick to the stomach, but he did not pass the information on just yet.

Then came a kind of accidental royal gift. On August 11, 2003 at 7 pm, Thailand's adored queen addressed the nation via TV, as she did annually for her birthday. She declared her love for Thailand and its people and also talked about her concern and sadness for the illegal wildlife trade that had been attracting some publicity at the time. Edwin felt that this was the impetus he needed to act.

Edwin went to see Swake Pinsinchai, who had been the provincial commander of the Royal Thai Police at the time of the murders at Highland Farm at Mae Sot the year before, and whom Edwin had had positive dealings with amid the human tragedy. He had moved on from Mae Sot and had been appointed the commander of the then-forestry police. Edwin had several other wildlife issues to raise and felt General Swake could be trusted. He gave over everything he had uncovered about the orang-utans.

Raids on Safari World occurred soon after. Edwin did not attend the first raid, but was present for the second to advise on handling the animals and assessing their condition. More than 100 baby orang-utans were found on the Safari World premises in 2003 and only four mothers, confirming the illegal importation suspicion. Alison and Jim Cronin from Monkey World in the UK had already given information about the orang-utan boxing.

"On reflection, I started rocking the boat before I had even properly put down an anchor," Edwin says. "I got involved in upsetting illegal wildlife traders way too quickly. But the Queen's speech was the absolute essential part of the action taken. Her grace and concern was the motivator to act."

Edwin thinks his agitation over Safari World and demands for the repatriation of the animals clearly extracted from the wilds of Indonesian Borneo added to the impetus for the raid of WFFT in 2012, because the management of Safari World was clearly well connected, given they had been allowed to continue operating without investigation.

Safari World, complete with orang-utan boxing shows that feature female apes dressed in bikini tops carrying around round cards and males kitted out in gloves and garish trunks, continues to operate today. At the time of the seizures, Safari World claimed they had acquired the apes through third-party suppliers and could not have known they were from the wild. The theme park continues to attest that their orang-utans are treated well.

Outrage burns inside Edwin like an all-consuming fire when it comes to wild animal mistreatment and the corruption that enables it to flourish. And the plight of orang-utans has often been the reason for his ire. In December 2008, he again got wind of the movement of the precious apes into a zoo. A contact, a foreigner in Thailand, told him that an order had been placed for three or four orang-utans with an illegal trader. The customer was a tiger and crocodile farm in Phuket that already had some orang-utans.

Edwin went to see for himself, posing as a European sex tourist, complete with a friend acting as his Thai 'girlfriend'. No one blinks at the sight of a big, blond European man with a young Thai girl in holiday spots.

He saw three orang-utans on display and viewed with his own eyes a room with about 10 more in tiny cages tucked at the back. He says they were clearly stressed and did not look to be in good health, and this worried him immensely. He used his contacts to establish they had not been registered and reported the matter to the Department of Natural Resources and Environment, sending them photos he had taken. There was no response within 30 days, so he reported it again. By now, he felt desperately concerned about the condition of the orang-utans.

"I called them and said to an officer I had had dealings with before that if they did not do anything, I would complain about their neglect to the administrative court," Edwin says. "He then called and said, 'We went in and all we found was goats in those same cages. No orang-utans. You were mistaken', and he sent me photographs of the goats. That just made me angrier. I said to him 'I sent you photographs of orang-utans in those cages. You had better find them or you really have a big problem'. I was furious."

Nine days later, the officer called Edwin, to say that they had found the orang-utans in cages on the side of a nearby highway.

They claimed there was no evidence of who owned them and therefore no lines of questioning to pursue. The apes were eventually taken to the government rescue facility at Rat Buri and were among the last group to be returned to Indonesia in 2015. The process of the seizure of the orang-utans – from Safari World and Phuket Zoo, as well as a couple from a police general's home in Vietnam and another from another in a private zoo in Chumpon province – was difficult because under Thai law it is not strictly illegal to have orang-utans. After all, they were not native to Thailand.

The first group was returned in 2007 and the last in 2015. WFFT had a hand in each intervention, but was never a part of their care because the Thai Government 'seized' them, and they were ultimately returned to the Indonesian Government, but the Foundation provided funding, logistics and financed and built all moving cages. It still upsets Edwin that the WFFT stickers applied to the hand-built cages were removed before the flights.

Edwin says he asked the Thai Government to allow WFFT to care for the beautiful, sentient apes as the negotiations were underway, knowing the animal welfare standards at his wildlife rescue centre were far higher than at a government facility, but they would not accede to his request. As always, the policy that any animal in Thailand that comes directly into government hands will never be given to an NGO to care for is ironclad until the proposed new laws are fully enacted.

Orang-utans are highly endangered. They are also highly intelligent, deeply sensitive and have complex social needs. Because they are so delightful and human-like, the international trade in orang-utan is almost always for them to be used in tourism or kept as pets.

"At that time when I was actively involved in returning them, I felt that if they were not repatriated, there were people who would benefit from the illegal trade, and that was something I could not tolerate. The system in Thailand sometimes has holes, and I was worried they would disappear through them again. Now I feel differently about their return, and I wish in some ways that I had not helped to send them."

The repatriations were repeatedly, enormously frustrating processes that involved delicate negotiations with the governments who had the orang-utans in their custody, and the nation to which the animals are native, Indonesia. And as with every situation like this, the creature is held in a kind of suspended animation until their status and future is determined. Government facilities are traditionally functional but achingly barren, with concrete floors, metal cages and no amusements. To a creature such as the orang-utan, which shares 97 per cent DNA with humans and whose intelligence and creativity are in plain sight, it is the equivalent of being an innocent sent to the worst kind of prison.

But Edwin believed it was all ultimately for their benefit and that if these striking, perceptive beings could endure the mental and physical anguish of the 'going-through' stage, they had a chance at being given a good life. He travelled with some of the shipments, including one that took 48 by now-teenaged orang-utans. On landing in Borneo, the military aircraft flight was met by 200 schoolchildren singing a welcome song on the tarmac. It moved him to tears, and he found himself on his knees, overcome with the beauty of the singing, and the emotion of the long struggle to get the orang-utans back where they belonged.

"At the time, I really believed that they could be rehabilitated at rescue centres in Borneo and Sumatra and released into the wild," Edwin says. "It felt right and noble; the proper thing to do. Also, importantly, I felt that if the orang-utans were not repatriated, they could still end up slipping through the government centres and ending up on the illegal wildlife market in Asia. That is no place for animals, especially those that have already suffered.

"For that reason, I felt very strongly that they should go back to their country of origin, but now I feel that we have failed them."

Edwin says the doors closed behind the orang-utans as they entered Indonesia, swallowing them into a silent, sapping abyss. Despite assurances before they left Thailand, there has been no news, no updates, and no acknowledgement. It is as if they have evaporated into the steam, the heat and the teeming masses of Indonesia. Now, more than 10 years since the first orang-utans were sent back, Edwin says he will not return any more.

"The Indonesian Government will not respond to my requests to know how they are doing now," he says. "They have never offered any recognition for all that we have done for those animals. It cost us a great deal of money, and I can't do any more at the moment because I can't be sure of what would happen to them, even though I know there are some still being illegally kept.

"Orang-utans are so, so similar to us, so in need of love and contact and freedom, and I can't be sure they have any of that. I feel I failed them and that I might have sent them off to a terrible life. I struggle with that, and I won't add more layers to my mistake.

"The information I have from contacts in Indonesia is that less than 10 per cent of them have been returned to the wild. Most of them are in zoos, not even in real rescue centres. I don't think we should spend any more time or money on helping to feed that market. It is disgusting to me that these beautiful animals should end up there."

Edwin fears the welfare and wellbeing of the orang-utans he returned are not of great concern in Indonesia. He says he can't dwell too long on the thought that he might have inadvertently tipped them from frying pan to fire, as would bring him undone.

But he has another chance to make orang-utan individuals' lives better. Two of these extraordinary, interesting, drastically endangered apes came in quick succession and by some strange twists into the care of the rescue centre.

On a warm day in February 2016, a blue and white animal carry case was seen outside the gate of the WFFT Wildlife Rescue Centre. This is not an unusual occurrence, and it was first thought the box contained one of many dogs or cats that are regularly dumped in the night. However, inside on this day was something far less ordinary.

Brown eyes that are remarkably human-like peered up. A dexterous hand clutched at an orange blanket and pulled it tight under a puckered chin; nimble fingers toyed nervously with sacking cloth within. In the box was a scared infant Sumatran orang-utan.

Edwin says he felt his heart melt on sight. The baby was beautiful, seemingly healthy, and she was all alone.

"I spoke to her. I told her it would be all right and that we would look after her," Edwin says. "I told her the worst of what she had been through was over now.

"There is so much about this animal that we don't know. We presume she came to us after a lot of publicity about an orang-utan called Milo who was being kept without a permit in poor conditions at Phuket Zoo and was seized. I think her owner probably panicked and was worried about prosecution for what they thought was illegally holding a similar animal. We presume her mother was murdered, because it is the only way to come by a baby orang-utan, the mother would have fought ferociously for her."

Orang-utans are the largest of the tree-living mammals and are native only to Borneo and Sumatra. Little Maggie, as she was named, had no one to teach her how to make a leaf nest at night, how to swing and forage, or perfect so many other necessary orang-utan skills. A long-term volunteer, Texan Shawn Kemp, was appointed as her primary carer, charged with researching her needs and delivering on her program of activities that would foster her wellbeing. Their bonding was important because at WFFT, Maggie was the only one of her kind.

But not for long.

In June 2016, the WFFT office took a call from a man who said he wanted to get rid of his 'pet monkey' and thought the rescue centre might be able to help him out. A date was chosen and when Edwin and his team arrived, the 'monkey' was revealed to be a Bornean orang-utan, with fine, ginger aerodynamic hair, mutton-chop sideburns and expressive amber eyes that spoke volumes. Chico had been bought as a baby for about 700,000 baht from an illegal wildlife trader. He was six years old, the owner said, and the owner was happy when Edwin agreed to take him into WFFT's care.

"I was a little startled when he started to hand over Chico's belongings: a little kid's go-kart, clothes including themed outfits, packaged snack foods that were full of sugar and starch, and human toiletries," Edwin says. "Chico had been treated as if he were a human child, and in my mind, there are not many things you could do that would be worse to a beautiful wild animal, particularly an orang-utan. To humanise an animal like that, to baby him, to make him into something so much less than he was born to be, a beautiful, strong orang-utan, was terrible."

Edwin says Chico's story was familiar: he was adorable as a baby, cute as a toddler and when the childhood years wore on and he effectively matured into a teenager, he became wilful and difficult. Such is the tumult of the 'in-between years' for all primates, including humans. And he was strong – so very strong. Chico's owner felt unable to handle him any longer and reached out to WFFT.

Chico was initially afraid of Maggie, possibly because it was the first time he had looked into familiar eyes since babyhood. Chico and Maggie now live in harmony in a one-hectare enclosure. They were primed for such a wide open space over two years when they would enjoy daily walks in the forest with Shawn, with whom they are extremely comfortable and regard as an authority figure. They were fed nutritious food, they were given spaces to explore and play, and they were given learning opportunities. And, importantly, they were taught to swing through treetops.

For now, the wildlife rescue centre at WFFT is a safe, stimulating, nourishing home to Chico and Maggie.

13. Freedom

The other apes at the WFFT wildlife rescue centre at Khao Luk Chang are far more obvious, if not always overtly visible. They call and they sing, providing the campus with the most earthy, melodious wild soundtrack that heralds every new day and sees it off again. The songs are awe-inspiring as if delivered directly from the soul of the world.

Six species of gibbons live at the Khao Luk Chang refuge, and they are, in an instant, enchanting to observe. Many are rescued pets, and these residents have charming but sad residual behaviours taught by their human keepers. One switches into a dance-floor groove at the regular sight of volunteers, who come twice a day to fill its food bowl or give it an enrichment activity, or at any of four daily water changes. Another sucks its thumb. Its neighbour might strike a pose or fiddle with its fingers in a particular way. The behaviours slowly fade as the time in care lengthens, as they begin to regain their natural actions and instincts, and learn that they are gibbons instead of human property.

Part of gibbons' appeal is that they are the only primates other than humans to be bipedal, or to walk erect on two legs. Their arms seem impossibly long, as if they are overstretched elastic, but this makes them perfect for swinging, an effortless, celebratory, air-borne dance of life. When they run, they must thrust the limbs skyward in a kind of comical surrender.

There are likely to be more than 1000 gibbons being illegally kept in Thailand, so appealing are these human-like beauties. Many of the gibbon species are endangered with the primary causes habitat loss, the illegal wildlife trade and use of body parts in Chinese medicine. Bizarrely, their flesh is even served to diners with palates for the exotic in niche wildlife restaurants in some Asian restaurants outside Thailand.

Gibbons at WFFT in many ways symbolise its precise ideal, because while the rescue centre has taken in countless animals of these species, it also has the chance to give the gibbons back to nature, with many family groups ultimately released into the wild.

The Gibbon Rehabilitation Centre at WFFT has carved a proud name for itself as often successfully traversing the long bridge to independence, with numerous gibbons being restored from being dependent house pets to wild animals. The transition is slow, with many having to re-learn to eat their natural diet, to sing and to swing. They need to learn the rules of interaction with their own kind, to forage and to protect themselves. They are progressively moved from individual cages, to pairs and to groups. The wildlife rescue centre now has 14 gibbon islands on the nearby lake and within constructed pools, which are a natural contained space because gibbons, like all other apes, do not swim. This is the last step of their rehabilitation and the only human contact is a visit from a boat to deliver food that complements their own foraging.

The ultimate, of course is freedom. When gibbons are released, the Thai Department of National Parks is involved, and they have found a second wild life near Mae Hong Son in past releases. It is then that their beautiful singing truly becomes a melody of absolute liberty.

But some gibbons that come into WFFT's care may not ever be able to live free lives.

Maami, a siamang, was a police officer's pet before coming to WFFT in 2007. The policeman was very bonded to her and her to him, and when he died of cancer, her human family felt they could no longer care for her in a way that was good for any of them. Maami has long, shaggy dark hair and an impressive throat pouch that enables her to release bellowing whoops and barks that can be heard in the nearby village and throughout the rescue centre grounds. She lives in a cage in the gibbon forest and has a particular dislike of large women, winding up with vigour at the sight of their approach.

Another gibbon resident is, sadly, far less lively. Jub Jib, a 15-year-old white-handed gibbon, came into WFFT's care in June 2017 after a lifetime as a house pet. She had worn diapers all the time, had clearly never seen grass nor gravel and did not sing or babble, much less swing. Her owners told vets at WFFT that they had had her since she was a baby, taking her in after her mother was caught in fighting between armed forces on the Thai-Myanmar border and fell from the forest canopy with her aboard. The mother died and the fall caused Jub Jib a severe head injury that left her with epilepsy.

When she came to WFFT, the little chocolate lady was dopey, her reaction times were painfully slow and her co-ordination was off. Her owners admitted they had dosed her with human sleeping tablets for the trip. But even when the effect of them abated, Jub Jib was scared of anything underfoot other than concrete, and it became evident she was dependent to the human anti-depressants her owners had given her to treat her epilepsy. She would not feed herself, but instead simply opened her mouth like a baby bird. Her bones were chalky, her muscle mass pathetic due to a lifetime of poor nutrition, lack of sunlight and the dearth of any exercise. She was tiny for her species and could not hang by her arms as a gibbon should. Her on-going rehabilitation involves daily physical therapies, but she will never be able to live independently.

But, as with all animals at the rescue centre, Jub Jib will be helped to re-find her instincts. She has been dragged from death's door and saved from further human harm, but the damage for her is pitifully lasting.

Animals confiscated by the government cannot come to WFFT under Thai law. The government does not work with wildlife NGOs in any structured or formal way on cases of abuse or neglect, but rather mostly tolerates the centres' activities and occasionally accepts an approach or offer to work on a specific joint project. The money for such projects comes from the NGO, but the benefit is Thailand's, and, of course, the animals'.

It is a part that Edwin plays willingly, arguing that the proper care of wild animals should never just be the exclusive realm of governments, but rather a collective, shared responsibility within any concerned community. Edwin is working with the government to build a bear rescue centre in northern Thailand, which the government will run. That WFFT wholly funds it is a sign of Edwin's good intent and desire to work together.

There are advanced plans in place to open a facility in which street dogs and cats will be spayed in Cha-Am, near the wildlife rescue centre. WFFT will fund and provide the building, employ a vet and assign volunteers to care for the temporary patients. The need is great in a city where street animals are prolific and Edwin says in doing this and offering the best of care, it shows that WFFT is invested in the health and wellbeing of all animals.

Edwin hopes that with the proposed new laws, the Thailand Government will embrace NGOs as partners in a holistic approach to rescuing wildlife and ensuring the nation's animals' health and wellbeing. This optimism is a giant leap from the fire and fight that consumed him when he began.

"When I look back, I suppose I saw myself as a renegade who kind of said 'fuck you' to the system and was going to rescue animals no matter what the rules were," he says. "I had that fighting approach in some of the rescues too. In the early years when I went to a rescue, I would see an animal in a terrible condition and I would talk to the owners and get angry and yell at them and tell them they were horrible people. And sometimes that made the person angry with me and decide not to hand over the animal. It did not help, and it took a while for me to see that.

"Now when I go to a rescue, I whisper in the ear of that animal, 'No matter what happened to you until now, I promise your life is going to change and your life will get better. That is my promise to you'.

"That works for me. The animal hears me. The animal is my focus, and I feel good about that. Instead of pissing off the owner, now I concentrate on connecting with the animal."

One of the worst cases of neglect Edwin came across was that of Joe, a macaque rescued by the WFFT team in 2016. Edwin led the mission, which began with a tipoff from a concerned foreigner about a monkey being kept in a gap between two buildings in a slum in central Bangkok.

"I have seen a lot of animal suffering, but I would say that the condition the monkey was kept in was probably in the top 10 of most horrible cases," Edwin says. "He had been in this tiny, dirty hell hole since 1991. That is 25 years with no clean water to drink, in almost complete darkness, alone except for visiting rats and in his own waste. His whole world was a 70x80x80cm box. It was truly horrible in ways I cannot describe. That he was still alive was almost unbelievable."

The owner was happy to give Joe up, telling Edwin he had the monkey come to him as a baby. In a story so often familiar in Thailand, Joe's mother had been killed by poachers, and all was well with the cute, playful Assam macaque for a time. He was a photographer's dream and a cute pet.

But when Joe hit adolescence, and hormones began to weave their strange, reckless spells, he became unpredictable and aggressive. It was then that the hole was created in which he would be harboured for the next 25 years.

The owner told Edwin he had made contact with Bangkok Zoo at one point but said they would only take Joe if the owner would pay for his upkeep. Nothing had happened since, and Joe's time in prison grew from weeks into years. Little by little, the cage was boarded up until only a corner was left for light, air and to pass food through. Joe was given junk food, packaged products and leftovers in an ad hoc manner. He could not climb or swing. He had no person or other animal to interact with; a desperate, isolating situation for such a social, sentient being.

"We sedated him and found that he was incredibly dirty and very weak, as his muscle tissue was almost gone; his teeth were rotting, and he was very dehydrated," Edwin says. "The slum was inaccessible for cars, so we had to carry him out to the local police station to register his rescue. I have been calling Thailand my home since 1990. I realised that for the entire time I had been living and working in Thailand, this monkey had been in that cage, waiting for someone to rescue him. I just wish we would have known earlier." Joe was housed in quarantine for many months, as his adjustment and rehabilitation were very slow. His nutrition had to be altered incrementally, his space expanded in stages; clean water was at first a strange curiosity. He was introduced to neighbours in abutting cages, the first time in a lifetime that he had heard, seen and come into contact his own kind.

Edwin says Joe's rescue elicited mixed feelings he had not felt so keenly before.

"I felt embarrassed to be a human being, seeing in this case what humans are capable of doing to an animal, but at the same time I was feeling proud to be a human because only a human could make a positive difference in this horrible case. It is the ultimate internal conflict: sick to my stomach but extraordinarily relieved."

In October 2017, Joe's restoration from human detritus to spirited monkey was as complete as it would be. First, Joe was moved to a side enclosure next to a macaque field for old ladies. Rose, Wan Jai and Jaw were observed interacting with him through the fence, so Joe was allowed into the field. The natural substrate of grass, trees, a pool, places to climb and places to hide had for so long been foreign to him, and he explored each thoroughly. Best of all, Joe, the monkey who had served more than a life sentence in a hellhole, was accepted by the troupe. For the first time since he was a baby, Joe had a family, and lived with them until his death from old age in January, 2019.

Edwin's approach to animal care, and his focus on minimising human contact and dependence, does not always make him popular with animal lovers.

"I am not one of these cuddly animal lovers who cries every time I see an animal suffering. I am one of these people who sees an animal suffering and thinks about what I can do for that animal or others like it. Is there a possibility to rescue it or alleviate its pain? Yes or no. If yes, then I formulate a plan. But I do not start battles I cannot win. There is no point in that, no point in broken hopes. It is very hard for people to understand that I cannot fight every battle."

Edwin says his approach and conduct are sometimes interpreted as cold or uncaring. It is neither; it is preservation and, in his book, shows respect for the animal. Similarly, people who first meet Edwin after learning of his wildlife work often expect someone softly spoken and alternatively dressed. Edwin is none of that. He can be hard in his expression and direct in what he says about the problems that he sees. Many people consider his delivery to be rude and abrupt, and when he does not act on what they think is required, they feel let down.

"Many times, people come to me and say 'Phuket Zoo needs to be closed because it is a shithole for animals'. And I say 'I agree with you, but the problem is that Phuket Zoo has a zoo permit; it legally owns the animals. There are no animal welfare laws I can use to close it down'. There are social media campaigns and pressures, but they have been tried in the past.

"The owner is still getting a lot of money from tourists making photographs with tigers and orang-utans. There is no way for that place to close unless the owner wants to end it. The best hope for places like that are if people stop going, stop taking photos and the owners give up their animals and try another business."

Edwin says of those who criticise him, the worst are sectors of the vegan community. Edwin is an omnivore who loves a good steak with his vegetables and bacon with his eggs. He has penchants for gorgonzola and gouda.

"It is an all-out attack sometimes. They say I cannot rescue an animal one day and then eat an animal or animal product the next. They call me a species-ist, a bigot," he says. "I can handle the criticism itself, but I feel this extreme judgment of others corrodes our collective cause because they are so vocal, so critical and that makes those people who are looking in at animal rescue think that we are all like that, that we are all extremists, which we are not."

Edwin says a case in point is Dominic Dyer, whom Edwin regards as a righteous fighter for animals in the UK. Dyer, the chief executive of the Badger Trust, policy adviser of the Born Free Foundation and author of a book Badgered to Death. The People and Politics of the Badger Cull, organises protests against the government-sanctioned badger slaughter, which has slain about 1000 badgers a year over five years. But extremist vegan groups called for a boycott of the protests purely on the grounds Dyer is not a vegan.

"The thing is, even if there is some point about human life being equal to all other living things, people in my position are expected to be more Roman than the Pope. We are expected to be saints because we rescue animals. But no one is pure and no-one can be all things.

"I was sitting in a bar a few years ago in Hua Hin with five or six of my volunteers, and there are girls there who were there to prostitute themselves. It is a common thing here; it is not as if we went to this bar because those girls were there because they are in every bar.

"One guy comes up to me and says: 'so this is where my donations go, to allow you to visit a whorehouse. You sit around girls who are being exploited while concerning yourself with animals being exploited. That is hypocrisy of the highest kind.' I said to the guy 'I have no fucking idea of who you are, and you do not know what you are talking about, but you are on the edge right now. And might I point out you are also in this bar, where these girls are. You have a few seconds to walk away or to apologise.' And he walked away."

On social justice issues, Edwin says the wires are too often crossed and that gives the world very confused signals. People must be able to have their personal space, and they must be able to be complexly human.

"The only reason I am not a vegan or vegetarian is because I am weak. I simply cannot do it," he says. "Being vegan would be unhealthy for me because I do not have the time to eat deliberately and that is needed if you cut out whole food groups that a human has come to require for health. I am always in a hurry; I am always grabbing food on the run around.

"But I think the lesson in all of this is that human beings have many parts and none of those parts is absolutely pure."

Edwin says apart from accepting the help extended by a select group, he has learnt to be as self-sufficient as possible. This fits with his nature which has always been to take the lead and carve his own path.

"Look at how I run my rescue centre. I don't want to beg with International Fund for Animal Welfare and World Society for the Protection of Animals with my head down and hands up. I don't want to rely on them for money," he says. "I want to do it in my own way, sustainably and generating our own Foundation's funds. And that has worked so well because I have the support of real people, not big organisations. The volunteers and individual donors are key."

WFFT builds infrastructure and improves management practices and facilities faster than any other organisation in the Thai wildlife sector.

"People criticise, and say I run my Foundation like a company, and it looks too much about business," he says. "My answer is 'are our animals better off, are they well cared for and do we rescue more animals than anywhere else? The answer to all those things is yes. The animals are at the centre of it all."

Edwin refuses to take donations from zoos or wildlife traders, despite offers in the past. He will not take funds from companies known to pollute the planet or that he ascertains have unethical, unsustainable practices.

Once again, he is proudly, intractably within and without – a renegade and a rule breaker in a sustainable world he has built around the object of his passion.

14. Sign O' the Times

In many ways, it is remarkable that Edwin is still alive, much less that WFFT is still not only operating, but blossoming.

Part of the reason is put down to Edwin's military-like discipline and street smarts; he is savvy enough to know where the safety lines lie and to sit with his toes touching but not over them most of the time. He knows the value of excellent contacts and has a detailed knowledge of the systems, both legal and in the shady spaces where light is rarely cast.

Since he began his animal rescue work and animal conservation involvement, Edwin has been under threat from those who don't like his interruption and agitation about illegal wildlife trade. He has been followed many times in his car to the extent where he keeps a weapon under the driver's seat.

He has had people turn up at the rescue centre, bellowing obscenities and screaming threats. One man who falsely accused Edwin of harbouring his confiscated gibbon lunged at him with a knife before fleeing the campus and then the nation. Edwin knew nothing of the animal; the gibbon had been seized by government officials and was therefore housed in a government facility.

Despite intermittent death threats from often-anonymous people, Edwin says he is rarely afraid of being killed by wildlife traders who are upset at his efforts to extinguish their lucrative operations.

"If I had been Thai, I would have been dead already," he says. "But the price on the head of a foreigner and a person with a high profile is too great. The media coverage it would get, and the fact that the police would be forced to really do something about it is enough to protect me. There are many Thais who have paid a far higher than me; they are the real heroes."

In recent years, much to his own surprise, this straight-talking, sometimes rude and always bold animal welfare and conservation campaigner has learnt the delicate art of diplomacy. Early in 2017, he found himself in the engine room of massive legislative reform around Thailand's animal laws, being given a seat at the parliamentary table, officially advising the Thai parliament law drafting committee on natural resources, animals and animal welfare.

The body concerns itself with the conservation of native wildlife, and also to bring in guidelines on animal welfare standards, control of contagious diseases and the management of wild animals perceived to be pests. Edwin had initially been invited to one-off consultations, asked to address the committee on two specific animal issues. Afterwards, he received a letter asking him to be a part of the committee wholly. It was a huge honour; he is the only non-Thai national on it, and it has brought him into close, regular contact with all the most powerful national authorities in the animal sector.

The parliamentary advisory committee meets each Wednesday which means Edwin is committed to making the six-hour round-trip journey to Bangkok every week, a big ask for one so manically busy and who sleeps as little as he does. But he has settled into the rhythm, using it as a time when he can play the music he loves in his sleek grey sedan as loud as he wishes, interspersed with taking and making business calls on his hand-free system. The weekly committee meetings are a commitment he sees as vital for his own and the animals' future, a big leap in a healthier direction that has potential to bring action instead of just more talk. It is the hope for something better that drives him.

"If you do not get involved in legislative reform you will sit here for 30, 40 or 50 years rescuing animals and not changing anything except for those individuals," he says. "The number of animals needing rescue will only rise. But if you work on legislation and rally for its enforcement and work on education you make a bigger difference. Every now and then, I feel very good about it. I see the shift in attitude in the public or the legislators, but every now and then, I also wonder if we are making any improvement at all."

Some of his despondency comes from the persistence of the use of wildlife in tourism. While in the West, awareness has been sharpened by social media campaigns to encourage travellers to resist parting with their holiday dollars at the expense of a chained monkey or an indentured elephant, huge numbers of visitors from nations such as China and Russia continue to feed the markets of pain and suffering. They attend places where animals are used apparently without thinking, encouraged by booking agents who pocket commissions and a culture that continues to see animals as props and amusements.

Agitators such as WFFT campaign for a behavioural shift in both users and operators. Where the animals involved in providing entertainment for financial gain are protected, and there are plenty of examples, even in the bigger tourist operations; arrests are only occasionally made.

"Even then a year later the same operators are back in the same business again in the same places, doing the same thing," Edwin says. "And sometimes the same police are involved. It is very frustrating."

Wildlife in Thailand has had a long history of having, at best, patchy care and protection.

In 2003, under pressure from the world and NGOs over the burgeoning practice of keeping wildlife as pets, the Thai Government issued an amnesty to offer people the chance to register and obtain permits for keeping native wildlife.

In Thailand, until 1992 wild animals were largely unrecognised, left lingering in a no man's land of existence without any real legal protection. Then the Wildlife Preservation and Protection Act was implemented, which offered a legislative lifeline to some species deemed valuable to the nation, but the framework around it was porous and the terminology vague enough that there were many loopholes and many gateways within.

Until recent years, species that were not native or on the Thailand's list of protected or reserved animals were still left open to exploitation and mistreatment. And of course, as ever, the illegal trade booms, bolstered and invigorated by paltry penalties and wishy-washy enforcement. But the laws Edwin is involved in shaping offer hope for something better, arguably the first legislation that demonstrates a real concern for the nation's wild animals and the future of the nation's precious, living natural resource. Strangely, the impetus for humane change was generated by a push on behalf of domestic creatures within the national borders.

Stray street animals are common in Thailand, and it is a centre of the dog meat trade, with businesses thriving on the movement of live canines to voracious consumer markets in China and Vietnam. The treatment of these animals is often brutal and cruel, with some being transported in bags and boxes with no food or water, often arriving dead or close to it.

Thailand had no specific legislation for acts of cruelty to animals, other than a minor offence that penalised it with a tokenistic 1000 baht fine. But cruelty was not defined, and the law was rarely enforced. Edwin is also on the animal welfare committee, which sits under the nation's livestock department. It meets monthly.

For 20 years, animal welfare groups lobbied the government, and with the advent of the internet, began to campaign globally to put pressure on the Thai Government to act against the barbarism. A mass protest of 30 animal protection groups outside parliament in April 2012 gained international media attention, and the government formed a sub-committee with representatives from the welfare organisations to prepare a draft bill to address the prevalent torture and abuse of dogs and other animals. While the absence of legal protections frustrated advocates for animal welfare for decades, once the wheels on this vehicle began to turn, it gathered speed quickly.

The framework for Thailand's first animal welfare law, the Prevention of Animal Cruelty and Provision of Animal Welfare Act, was passed on December 26, 2014. It was intended to stop the illegal meat trade, but there was an overall positive kicker for other animals too; it was also the first time animal owners were compelled to provide basic standards of care and shelter for those in their custody and importantly, it offered some protection for wildlife and animals stolen from the wild. These precious animals were ignored until WFFT and the Thai Animal Guardians Association agitated for their inclusion.

Animals raised as pets or used for work or performance must not be caused to suffer and must be housed and fed appropriately. The Act prohibits the neglect, torture and reckless transporting of live animals, and has teeth, up to a year in jail or a fine of 40,000 baht for offenders.

Until the Act passed, any animal that was not native to Thailand and was not on a list of reserved or protected animals was not offered protection. It means that people could buy a kangaroo, a macaw or another species from another nation and the animal had no welfare, treatment or cruelty protections. Under the new law, of course, animals on the CITES list are also included, so keeping animals protected and endangered in other nations is now also illegal in Thailand. That takes in tens of thousands of animals.

"We have for a long time had a list of what is banned and what is allowed, but up until now we have not had anything dictating how animals must be kept," Edwin says. "And we still have much to work on in the detail; how much land they need or what standard of nutrition should be a minimum. That is occupying me now; that is what I am working with the parliamentary committee on.

"It is one very good thing is that some people high up in the department of National Parks are with me on this. I also told them that we need to think about this very quickly because the time will come when we have regulation, and there will not be people who can keep animals anymore because they can't keep up the standards expected under law."

In serving on the parliamentary committee, Edwin feels he has grown a great deal. He says he has learnt to listen more and talk less, and how to put his case in ways that are more palatable to others, where before his approach was more to hit them squarely between the eyes.

"With my work in Parliament, I think I have finally lost the kid in me whose first instinct was always to say 'I don't care. I will do it my way'," he says. "It is quite a formal process, and I think it is good for me personally to engage in it every week. I am still being the funny guy, the rebel and the joker, but I know now when to shut up and be serious. I have even learnt to be diplomatic when necessary. That might be a huge surprise to those who know me."

And while Edwin is unique in being the only foreigner at the table, he also has another insight into how the previous legislation works and what could be improved in the administration of it. Bitter experience has informed and shaped him.

"Nobody knows more about the wildlife laws than I do," he says. "I have been on two sides of it; as one who helped craft its shape and one who was charged under it. I have also studied in depth what other nations do. I know the loopholes really well because I have used them myself in the past."

The detail is continually being hammered out, because the process of law reform in Thailand is long and detailed, with layers, particulars and approvals stretching over years. The bulk of the law was in place before the elections in 2019.

One section of the new Act has thrown a hand of hope out to Edwin and those who work for animals. An article under the Wildlife Preservation Act says that if the government sees fit, or does not have the ability to care for an animal, others may be appointed to step into the breach and help them with that creature's care. This is a legal first, and Edwin hopes WFFT and other ethical wildlife NGOs will eventually be called on.

The legal position of many in the Thai Government has always been that NGOs are only in the wildlife care sector to line their own pockets. This is a frustratingly intractable view that Edwin has been unable to shift, no matter how hard he has tried.

"For them to say that is like me saying that no government official cares about the wild animals and that all government facilities are pieces of shit," he says. "That is not true and neither is what they say about NGOs. It is offensive, because I do not benefit from rescuing and caring for wildlife; it is the animals that benefit. That is what we are all about: the animals. But no matter how loudly I say it, how many times or who I say it to, the idea that all NGOs are preying on animals and using Thailand's wild animals for their own benefit seems to stick. It pisses me off over and over again. Not all NGOs are the same, and neither are all government officials. We have rotten apples in both barrels."

The problem under law is that NGOs are outsiders. They must officially register that they have taken a wild animal into their care, but the government can swoop in at any time and take it into their own facilities. Edwin knows this only too well, having been raided so dramatically in 2012.

"I have had my staff make presentations to the official bodies about how effectively a cohesive approach works in other nations, but so far, there has been resistance," Edwin says. "The thing is that it would take the pressure off the government to be solely responsible. It effectively makes less work for them and costs them less because the NGOs pay and take on the duty – and do it better. The NGOs also do it quicker because they are not restrained by bureaucracy, and most dumped or surrendered wild animals do not have time to wait for government processes to be followed because they are sick or injured and in need of care immediately, or they are at risk of dying or worse.

"I deeply believe that the government should spend their money on protecting animals in the wild – in situ conservation – instead of setting up more facilities to take in seized animals, particularly animals that have no value to conservation whatsoever," he says. "Taxpayers' money should not be spent on those facilities when they exist already, but have not been set up by the government."

Edwin says the government facilities are incapable of caring for all the rescued wild animals that are currently in the care of NGOs in Thailand. The government centres simply do not have the physical capacity or financial means, as evidenced in the Tiger Temple raid of 2016. The tigers seized then are still languishing in tiny cages or have died there.

"As a matter of fact, all NGOs together couldn't deal with the numbers or the need either," Edwin says. "It is only by working together that we can make a real difference and care for these animals properly. I will do everything I can to work towards and be a part of that model to show it works. I have great hopes that we will achieve this eventually."

The irony of the government seeking Edwin's counsel and drawing on his long experience with wildlife rescue and care while simultaneously threatening to stop his work is rammed home regularly. Edwin is frequently the recipient of letters from officials, warning him to stop taking in rescued and surrendered wildlife and threatening him with seizures.

And bizarrely, those warnings have ramped up since his involvement in the parliamentary committee. In June 2017, Edwin received a letter, saying the government was soon going to take custody of 208 animals cared for at WFFT. He staved off that seizure with the support of his contacts in high places. In November 2017, he was again told that all the registered animals would soon be taken. While the receipt of such communiqués rattles him and makes him burr up, he has become used to having to quickly rationalise and seek a way to quell the impending threat. Mostly, he has developed a pattern of not responding reflexively to the documents and to keeping his head down until he is forced to enter the fray.

The government knows at all times how many animals are in WFFT's care, because of the requirement to register each rescue. The wildlife rescue centre is forced to effectively tip off a system that is designed to undo them and dismember their work. In essence, they are forced to load the gun that can be used against them at any time.

"It has never worked well. We have never had a period of calm and working together," Edwin says. "I am always looking over my shoulder, waiting to be hit again from behind. It is never from the front. I do not know one NGO in Thailand that is happily, comfortably working with the government on the care of animals or wildlife. Not one."

In the midst of the constant tension of threats to remove those animals that have found refuge, Edwin says he must focus on looking ahead, working towards solutions rather than being weighed down too long by the problems. Edwin wants minimum standards for those setting up rescue centres, which also come under the only available category for the legal keeping of wildlife – zoos.

Oddly, WFFT has been forced to lodge an application for registration as a zoo, even though they are far from the standard world perception of what a zoo facility is. In Thailand, there are many registered zoos that are not open to the public or set up as amusement parks, including tiger farms. Under law, there is no other category available for those who keep wild animals, and Edwin laments that there should be a classification for rescue centres and shelters to set them apart from those keeping animals for financial gain. But his hands are tied.

WFFT's zoo permit application took an extraordinary amount of time to process, presumably held up by those Edwin had crossed swords with in the past.

The wildlife rescue centre at Khao Luk Chang consistently aims to adjust and update to maintain the highest wildlife care and welfare standards in Asia. There is pride in that for Edwin and Tommy, not because it is impressive to the officialdom but because it means the animals there are living under the best possible conditions. In contrast, Edwin says that under current animal welfare laws in Thailand, the government should be arrested for breaches in some of its own rescue and breeding facilities. The enclosures and cages are generally tiny, the nutrition provided to the animals is very basic and the lack of stimulation has potential to drive an intelligent animal mad.

"Anyone can see it for themselves. Anyone can go and see that this could be so much better if only they would adopt some of the practices that have been proven to work in places such as ours," he says. "What is offered now is simply not good enough.

"It gives me hope that there is an awareness of this now among some key people, but I don't see that there needs to be bigger or more government facilities; they just need to work with the best of the NGOS and support them in taking care of the animals that the government takes. The accommodation and facilities are already there, just not with the Thailand Government labels on it."

Edwin's work in formal circles to try to improve the standards for animals and framework for their rescue ventures far from the meeting rooms of Parliament. He is the secretary-General of both Wild Animal Rescue Network and Wildlife Friends International. He is the co-founder of a new organisation concerned with dog and cat welfare, People and Animals Thailand.

Edwin registered WARN as a foundation in The Netherlands in 2014. It is a collective of 44 NGO wildlife rescue centres and wildlife protectors in Asia that shares knowledge and information on animal care, rescue strategies, team building and administrative approaches. Not everyone is included, and the group prides itself on aiming for and implementing world's best practice in wild animal care and management. Only those with high ethical standards and are allowed in.

"If you are a petting zoo or a tourist attraction, you can forget it," Edwin says. "It is an elite group by design because we needed to pull together those who want to move forward sustainably in approaches to wild animal rescue in Asia. It has generally been a very good initiative for all of us."

In formal terms, Edwin's transition to wildlife rebel to adviser to the power elite is largely complete. In many ways, at the start, he was 'the man least likely' but with maturity has come recognition that the deepest, longest lasting changes must come by burrowing within and working from the inside. He may still be a renegade at heart, a rascal in the day-to-day, but when animal lives are in the balance, even Edwin has learnt to walk some lines.

Broadening opportunity knocked unexpectedly in 2015, when WFFT entered a memorandum of understanding with Mekong Wildlife Limited, the owners of the Laos national zoo near Vientiane. It seems like a strange departure for a conservationist and anti-zoo activist, but there was method in the madness. Edwin was to facilitate the construction of the nation's first wildlife rescue centre within the grounds.

Mekong Wildlife Limited is one of the companies run by Eddie Kiasrithanakorn, who also is the Asian manufacturing licensee for Honda motorbikes and owns a number of hotels. Before the region was torn apart by the Vietnam and Laos conflicts in the 1970s and businesses were nationalised, the entrepreneurial family also had the now-widely known Beerlao company in its portfolio. Like so many others in conflict zones, they were forced to flee as refugees, in their case to Australia, but returned later and remade their fortune.

The agreement was that the zoo, which was bleeding money due to poor ticket sales and rapidly-decaying, inadequate enclosures, would continue to operate parallel with the rescue centre for the time being. Edwin employed a vet and fitted out a mini hospital. The Foundation developed a necessary quarantine area and paid for everything that goes with the management of volunteers including their accommodation and co-ordination, and paid for the running of the rescue centre. Mekong Wildlife employed managers for operations and construction after these were selected by WFFT.

The step was strategic in Edwin's war on illegal wildlife trading, and he felt it was vastly important for the wild animals in that nation which is renowned as a channel through which illegal wildlife passes en route to China. The combination of official corruption and grinding poverty make it a market ripe for illicit trades to flourish.

"Until 2015, I looked at the wildlife trade from one side of the border. You could intercept sometimes before the animals crossed, but basically once they were gone, that was it," Edwin says. "Now we were on the other side as well. If the traffickers were not intercepted in Thailand, we could intercept them in Laos and take the animals into our facility if necessary.

"I have had eyes and ears in Thailand for more than 16 years, but once we got involved in Laos, I had eyes and ears on the other side of the border and hands too because we were there."

This hope struck pay dirt on occasion, including in December 2016, when the Foundation was called on to care for and rehabilitate, and ultimately release, a truckload of 165 pangolin caught on the Laos side of the border with Thailand.

The involvement in Laos paid off in another way. Edwin was invited to be a part of an NGO-government advisory group to the Laos government, offering technical support on wildlife management. After 18 months working with the nation, Edwin felt he had been accepted and was starting to have input on their wild animal laws, too.

For a time, the zoo-rescue centre agreement worked relatively well. The existing run-down facilities improved little by little. Groups of bears and macaques, at least, were moved fairly quickly into open fields from their tiny, crowded cages.

But Edwin always kept his eyes on the bigger prize.

"My ultimate goal would have been to have the zoo component close down and turn it into an education centre. The company we were in partnership also initially expressed the desire to do that," he says. "But it was very hard to attract sponsorship and money into the project, because it is not seen as particularly glamorous. It was also remote – not near a village in the same way as the Thailand rescue centre is – which made it difficult to attract volunteers."

A year before Edwin came to the arrangement with Laos Zoo, he had a little spate of running drones over the Thai border into Laos. He and a drone specialist received images of tiger farms from which they could assess their size and operation. A farm they surveyed was one that Edwin believed had supplied the Tiger Temple. During one such surveillance operation, the farm's security team started shooting at the drone.

"The problem with that incident was that you have to land the drone where you are, pick it up and get the hell out of there," he says. "It is too expensive just to leave. The landing, getting it into the car and getting away provided a few heart-stopping moments, even in a sparsely populated area. Perhaps that was because it was during the day and people don't want you looking; we were white faces and we stood out."

A three-metre high wall surrounded the compound, and it was patrolled by guards armed with automatic weapons. The acrid smell of tiger faeces had been noted emanating from there, but there was no other way to look in other than with a drone. They found the evidence they sought using the flying machine in combination with GPS trackers on vehicles.

"I had to be sure for myself. I could not go on reports of others before I wrote a media release. I did not want to endanger those giving me information, and I needed to know for sure that if I said there were 400 tigers in there by seeing it for myself. Many other NGOs make claims without knowing for sure.

"That incident cemented for me the need to get into Laos, to get deep inside it and become a part of it, so that we could work from within for the animals there as well."

Although Thailand is a military regime, Edwin knows it inside out. He knows how the police operate, how the government works. He knows the cultural sensitivities that guide what he can and cannot say. He did not know these things with Laos, a vastly different culture, in the beginning. It is a volatile mix of strict ancient traditions with modernity knocking at the door via China. Gravel roads with axel-breaking potholes are driven on by a fleet of brand new cars bought with generous government credit offers. Tumble-down houses stand next to French-inspired palaces. Coca-Cola is sold alongside live wild animals in the markets. And everywhere is the presence of rich, red earth.

A communist country with an unelected government, the government and police have unlimited powers with no checks and balances. If the police say you are wrong, you go to jail, particularly as a foreigner. Village chiefs still have the rights of exclusion from village borders or jailing those who offend them.

"It is in many ways a very difficult country," Edwin says. "But I really wanted to be part of the changes on wildlife protection there in the long-term. It took a lot of educating myself because I had to be very clear that the modus operandi there was different.

"In Holland, I can speak my mind, and they can go to hell if they don't like it. In Thailand, I have to put a golden edge around it and soften it. But with the Laotians, I had to tell half the truth, or the truth in two parts, because I didn't want to get into trouble."

The relatively small population size of Laos and simple administrative structure also had advantages. Edwin says he was in a position where he could access a Lao minister or senior official directly. In Thailand, it takes more work.

In 2015, after approaching the Laos Government about starting a wildlife rescue centre, Edwin was told they did not need one. But in 2016, the Laos Department of Natural Resources made a statement at the CITES conference in South Africa that they were going to close the tiger and bear bile farms and work towards sustainable practices for wildlife.

"To be honest, I think the Laos Government simply made that statement to relieve the pressure a little. It certainly has not happened yet. I think they just wanted to be seen doing the right thing. I think there will be animals disappearing into the market before they start confiscating the animals and closing the farms. I predict there will be no animals to rescue by the time that is done because the animals will have been illegally traded. I think that they are playing the time game which in plain English is called bullshit."

Edwin believes there are at least 100 bears still in these farms, maybe as many as 200. He has attempted to take custody of the bears, but whenever he has tried to get dates and times for serious discussions, the right people to talk to are unavailable.

"The UK Government and EU delegations have even offered money to put an end to this, but the Laos Government always insists that the money come to them, and they will co-ordinate the closure. No sensible organisation or delegation would even be a part of that double-handed, opaque way of doing things."

One of the most active organisations on the ground in Laos, Wildlife Conservation Society, has offered to co-ordinate the move to close the bear bile farms, and still the government has refused. A massive cultural shift in approaches to wildlife care and management might be needed but is a long way off, and Edwin saw the opportunity to partner with Laos Zoo as a way of leading by example. WFFT spent about $US100,000 on establishing and running the centre. They funded, among other things, the volunteer co-ordinator position, medical facilities and supplies, office equipment, cameras, fridges and washing machines. WFFT built a website and social media spaces. But after two and a half years, in November 2017, Edwin withdrew from involvement in the centre. He was tired and frustrated, exhausted by endless blockages and delays.

He says the move away from operating as a zoo and increasing the wildlife rescue component was too slow for his comfort level. There were intractable disagreements and communication breakdowns with the wildlife rescue centre managers in place there. The agreement had been that he would advise on wildlife matters, and he was rarely consulted or informed about their operations. Edwin says he is very sad for the animals at the centre, whom he had hoped to be able to give better, long lives in big, open spaces in the same way as he has achieved in the Thailand wildlife rescue facility. He says he would be open to future opportunities in wildlife rescue in Laos.

"We also had a memorandum of understanding with the owners; we had no contract. It was a gentleman's agreement, and I would never make that mistake again. Partnerships need a properly vetted contract because if you have a falling out over an issue and you do not own the land on which your volunteers labour, and the infrastructure and equipment you provided sit, you have nothing."

Edwin also admits that working with a partner in a wild animal rescue facility was not instinctively easy for him. He is used to running things in his way, on his terms, and with only his Foundation, his conscience and the animals to answer to.

15. Don't Dream It's Over

From the outside, WFFT looks like a hive, humming with productivity.

Within, it is busy, vibrant, and like the animals it serves, very much alive. The life force of the campus is the army of international soldiers, who labour and sweat for the good of the animals. They are the lifeblood that keeps the engine of hope running, and Edwin says he would not be able to run his rescue centre without the volunteers' many hands.

"You can spend a lot of money on beautiful enclosures for our 700 animals – that is ideally what we want to do – but we also have to maintain the housing and facilities for the volunteers," he says. "The Thai climate is not kind and the need for maintenance is constant to keep the rooms at even a basic standard. We have to be sure they are fed well, too. We have to care for both animals and volunteers because both are very important to the Foundation."

Edwin says he feels satisfied that his centre offers the mostly-young people a chance to develop themselves, to be stretched in the physical work and to broaden their minds. But he sees a young generation that is uncertain of the future, that is collectively less directed than those that went before.

"The world is changing rapidly, and their absolute dependence on social media is frightening," he says. "It does a great disservice to democracy and our culture because it spreads half-truths and misunderstandings. There are no checks and balances. At least when I watch Fox, I know I am being fucked around by Republicans, and when I watch CNN, I know the Democrats are behind it. That is OK. But on Facebook or Twitter I get things thrown at me that are pure lies, and I am not the only one. And people just believe what they read is the truth as if we're in some kind of mediaeval time."

Social media has certainly been a good vehicle for spreading awareness of the work WFFT does, but there is so much information, such a constant stream, that Edwin feels consumers lose sight of the important information because of the sheer volume, the blasting noise of posts and tweets. He says 200,000 followers could mean nothing and could mean everything, but it is hard to gauge how engaged those followers are or even if they are real people.

"People who say that social media brings in funds are lying. There is no way to know that. For all the likes and supportive words, I do not see that translating to on-the-ground, real support, real action," he says.

He says the time of rapid change also extended to economies and lifestyles. He believes the time of superiority in the West was coming to an end.

"One thing the refugee issues and mass migration have brought people in the West is the realisation that there are people in the world who are willing to work twice as hard as they are, that the wealth and status we currently have in comparison to other parts of the world is going to turn around," he says.

"For example, The Netherlands is one of the 20 richest countries in the world generally, but in 15-20 years that is not going to be so because they do not produce much anymore. They trade, they have service industries, but compared to India, China, Indonesia and Thailand where people are willing to work 70 hours a week, they want to work 37 and if possible far less. How can you expect to still become richer when you are not willing to work harder and longer?"

While he is irreligious, Edwin says he has spent his life trying to make meaning of it, and at times, this has been developed through a process of deciding what he does not want. But he says the desire to live a meaningful life has driven him – that and the act of working hard on something purposeful.

"They work hard here in Thailand. They might work 14 hours, but they sleep well. Once they put their heads down on the pillow, they sleep because they are not worried as us from the West are. Last night, I slept for five hours because I worry. I envy Thai people for only one thing; their ability to sleep anywhere at any time. I simply can't do that."

Edwin has had rarely a solid night's sleep for a decade, but he thinks his sleep disturbance probably started when his parents separated 40 years ago.

His agile brain has always been hard to lull into a state of rest, with the wheels ever turning and the list of things to do growing. There have been times when his utter exhaustion has brought him to the brink of feeling like he was losing his mind.

During the day, he often resembles a whirling dervish, jumping from one task to another or juggling several at once. In conversation, he is animated and strident, but often one exchange is spliced into another and few are ever completed in one sitting. His phone is endlessly ringing and beeping. But he dismisses the ideas of meditation or similar practices as being suitable to help him quiet his mind.

"As I see it, if I can't sleep stretched out on a soft bed in a quiet place, how can I be calm in a yoga position? I tried it once, and it made me laugh," he says.

His witching hours start at 2 or 3am, when he surfaces from sleep, usually as a result of a nightmare, and finds his mind is spinning before his eyelids bat open. His thoughts run here and there, his awareness on high beam. Matters of business and of the heart – loves, truly – are suddenly his enemies in the inky night. Rarely does proper sleep find him again. At times, he is so tired during the day that he struggles with words, with co-ordination and with continuum of thought. He says if there is an afterlife – and he doubts that – he hopes he can just find a place to rest there.

Edwin's health is not always good. He has high blood pressure, a condition that is partly genetic and partly exacerbated by lifestyle. He is regularly heavily medicated for depression and the side effects can be very unpleasant. He says he feels like a zombie sometimes.

"I am one of those people who, when I drink, I don't stop until I drop, the bar closes or the money runs out. Same with the gym: I am all or nothing. I feel better in my mind when I exercise, but I am either doing it a lot or not at all," he says.

The depression came over him like an unexpected wave. At a conference in Phnom Pen in 2014, he first found himself feeling very tired, and he had a sense of disorientation and dizziness. He stopped drinking alcohol for perhaps the first time in his adult life to try to shake it, but the feeling did not abate. Then he was woken in the middle of the night, clutching his chest in what he felt sure was a heart attack.

"We went to the hospital, and it was a shit experience," he says. "The Cambodian hospital was shocking, like a hospital of nightmares. They did all kinds of tests, but they could not find anything wrong with me. When I flew back to Bangkok, I saw my own doctor, who ran tests and told me my heart was fine."

A couple of weeks later, in Bangkok, Edwin had a similar experience: chest pain, breathing difficulties, muscles tensed all over to the point of cramping. It was an out-of-body feeling, and Edwin was ultimately found to be suffering from severe anxiety. He recalled being in Europe a year earlier, when he developed a red circle on his back, like he had slept on a coin. He reasoned the irritated circle was a reaction to a bite from a bug or a tick. He had fevers and headaches and pain in his bones, but he had written it off as an overreaction due to stress. Subsequently, yet another doctor completed a thorough physical and mental check and told Edwin he thought he had Lyme's Disease. He said it could affect the mind, the brain, and depression and panic attacks were quite common.

"When you are missing an arm or you have cancer, people feel sad for you. But when it is unseen, it is different. Anxiety is an illness, but people just think you are nuts. It can be treated and you can live with it, but it is difficult to manage," he says.

"I have always thought a lot about death. I used to dream about it a lot as a kid. It used to frighten me, but the older I get, the more I think of death as the time when I will rest, when I will get a good sleep. Most of the time, I am just so very tired."

The panic attacks can be as debilitating as they are inconvenient. Edwin has had several at the big, bulk-order supermarket Makro, triggered when he reaches for something he expects to be in a familiar place and finds it is not there. He says he first feels confused, then he looks around and feels panic that he does not recognise anyone around him even though he logically knows they are strangers. Suddenly he gets dizzy and gripped by maddening fear and has to get out. The lack of control is terrifying.

While the incidents occur most at night as he closes his eyes, Edwin says if he has a panic attack in a public space, he removes himself and once it passes, he returns.

"It is part of that never-give-up thing. I won't let it beat me. I always go back and finish what I was doing before being rudely interrupted," he says.

The depression has come in waves, most often when he is very run down or particularly tired. It is worst when he feels beaten down after a conflict or when he feels distant from those who are important to him.

"I realised that if I kept going as I was, I was going to kill myself again," he says. "I killed myself in a way with the car accident because I was working too hard and living too hard in ways that did not make me happy. But I was only 34 years old then, and at 53, I feel that if I can't step back from some things I will not be able to continue.

"I think a lot. I worry even when things go well, because I think 'shit, what happens when it changes, when it doesn't?' It is almost as if I cannot let myself enjoy success, and that I can't enjoy the good things I have done.

"There is no reason for it because since I got out of the army, overall things have only got better in my life. There have been ups and down of course, but even when I am down, I consciously think this is an opportunity for a fresh start. When I lost everything in 2000, I felt relieved I did not have to pay 300 salaries or the invoices on the desk anymore. In the two years that I lived upcountry in Khao Krapuk after that, I learnt more about Thailand than I had in the 10 years before. If I look back, there has been a general upward trajectory, so there is no logic to the negative feelings."

Edwin has two brain specialists looking after him. One says his mental health condition is very straight forward and delivers medication and the other wants him to see a psychiatrist in addition to the measures he already undertakes. He refuses, so she refuses to prescribe him medications. It is a standoff Edwin is cranky about.

"I refuse to see a shrink. I don't need someone to tell me I am nuts; I already know that," Edwin says with a wink. "I think when I was younger, I just handled things, but now I am older, I think maybe my mind has got away from me. Sometimes, I can't control or refocus in a way I am used to when I begin to feel the stresses."

Edwin admits his personal style and delivery is abrupt, but as he has grown older, he feels less apologetic about it. Demanding people tire him; people who tell him what he does wrong bore him. But he is also trying to change his approach.

"I have learnt in the past few years, probably since the raid in 2012, that I can't control every part of everything. I have come to a state of mind where that control freak part of me that I had through my life had to be let go," he says. "I realised I can't be on top of all things at all times. Eventually, bit by bit, that has happened. I think the decision to ask Tommy to come back and to take over much of the operational decision-making was part of that."

Edwin says he has never been able to trust anyone with decision-making as much as he does Tommy. He simply could not keep juggling it all. In addition to the massive responsibilities of the Foundation, he drives up to 150,000km a year, and in 2017 alone made five overseas trips.

Tommy and Edwin are the odd couple in many ways. Tommy is 20 years younger than Edwin, is warm and generally has an engaging, ingratiating way with people. Both men have booming voices, love a joke, and lose their cool in spectacular fashion from time to time. The pair's interactions oscillate between intensely serious to flippant and sarcastic. In both forums, it is punctuated with personal, sometimes harsh jokes. They are a good team and good friends.

"I could not do this without him," Edwin says. "I honestly couldn't because I trust him, and we work well together towards this common purpose. "

Tommy is an early riser and Edwin generally eases into the day after his always-broken nights. Tommy is also a circuit breaker between the staff and Edwin, dealing with the on-the-ground, day-to-day issues that can be both mammoth and numerous. Edwin is calmer now, and the staff is happier since Tommy came back, because Tommy has the human touch and patience that Edwin often lacks. Being the in-betweener can sometimes put Tommy in a position akin to being in a washing machine and a tumble dryer all at once

"I listen," Edwin says vehemently. "I might not agree with Tommy and I might do what I was going to do anyway, but I do listen. We might have big fights and might say harsh things, but that is my way, perhaps. The funny thing is the Tommy usually agrees with me. I explain why, and usually he will agree."

Edwin says he wants to remain in charge of the Foundation for as long as he can partly because he feels responsible for seeing through the donors' intentions. Trust perhaps becomes more precious in a sometimes-untrustworthy land. Regardless of how his gruff and direct exterior is viewed, Edwin is unusually inclusive of people with difference. Seven of his staff members are aged over 65. He has had many openly gay members of staff, some are gender fluid and a range of nations is represented.

"People are people to me," he says. "What I do not like is when they use an attribute as an excuse, or they wave it in my face. I have people working with me and among my friends because I want them there, period."

Edwin would love to see more people adopt the tourism model of elephants being able to be observed roaming free without direct human interaction.

"I will never understand why people slag others off when they are successful. Why not copy them or even better, copy and improve? I would be so happy if people copied me because it would be better for the animals. They would have a better life."

The newest addition of land, temporarily called Project 4, is 20 ha on which, eventually, 20 elephants will wander. There is a lake and hills, scrub and trees, meaning there is enough variety in the elephants' environment to provide amusements and interest, and enough space so that they can navigate their own social circles. Several gibbon islands have also been created in this new landscape. A block of beautiful new rooms is perched there too, offering paying guests views of elephants roaming and playing in the broad, natural expanse.

The increasing numbers of day-trippers who mostly come from Hua Hin and Cha-Am to the centre are able to see the animals from open-sided buses. Diners watch them from a well-placed restaurant and viewing platform. It is a win-win situation as far as Edwin is concerned, and he feels satisfied that this part of the operation has expanded in a sustainable way. The previously-built Eco Lodge, which features elevated guest bungalows that are perched at the edge of a lush, wide open enclosure where a trio of elephants meander at their leisure, is another part of this model.

"It works; it really does. Some say to me that I should be ashamed because the elephants are still being exploited," he says. "But isn't the ability to observe elephants in a natural environment where they are doing what they want to in a space that is interesting and stimulating to them, a positive exploitation? Doesn't it help understanding and appreciation of them without anything required of the elephant? I believe it does."

Edwin says there are few he admires in animal-focused tourism in Thailand, but one is Lek Chailert, who owns Elephant Nature Park in Chang Mai.

"I think Lek has done great things, and her profile is very high, but she is a one-woman show. If she dropped dead tomorrow, her organisation would be in serious trouble," he says. "If tomorrow I die, everything would keep going. As a matter of fact, it would probably bring in more money. With Lek, they would be worried about whether it would continue.

"Elephant Nature Park is a very good organisation, very professionally managed. She makes big money, but we have a different philosophy – one of their objective is to breed in captivity. We do not. They are focused on education through tourism. I only want around 60 day trippers a day because I do not want WFFT to turn into a zoo. But yes, we are both about helping animals."

But there are operators who are not registered foundations. They are sole operators in effect, but operate as large organisations. There is no ethical or business framework and Edwin says this is very concerning.

"I wonder why some of these people who set themselves up and buy an elephant and appeal for funds on social media don't join a group that has lasting experience and form on the board. I wonder why they must go alone and set something up in their own name?" he says. "I have to believe they do not have the animal at the heart of their motivation, that they need their own name in there and their own ego involved. There are so many who want to be the Jane Goodall of the elephants in Thailand; they just want to make a name."

In Edwin's view of things, in the same ways as you cannot say that all people in Thailand are lazy, or all Australians are alcoholics, you cannot say that all animal lovers or those who rescue animals are good people.

"For me, from the beginning, I had a plan. But I was 34 when I started. I already spoke the language. I knew the country, and I knew the law. I was much better prepared than most of those who come in from outside and want to save wildlife here. My dream became a target because I had a plan. That is the difference between my set up and others, and it is a very important one."

Recently, his model and advice has been sought from further afield. Edwin is now advising Stichting Leeuw, a Dutch organisation, the representatives of which attended a presentation Edwin was invited to at ABN AMRO Bank in The Netherlands. Their refuge for lions and tigers will soon include elephants rescued from Europe's circuses after animals were excluding from the fanfare and spectacle of the big tops. The consultation took Edwin back to Holland many times in 2017 and 2018 and may ultimately result in him soon being able to bring some of Thailand's elephants and tigers back where they belong.

Edwin has already visualised and earmarked land that will feature a spectacular series of enclosures to accommodate the rescued tigers and enable people to observe them moving freely.

Edwin's global vision is cast in other directions too, towards trying to stem the flow of the huge numbers of animals needing refuge, with many being deposited at the end of a series of steps that starts with the illicit trade in wild animals. To get to the core of the issues, he realised early that he could not always rely on the information of others and needed to undertake his own investigations. Funding for something so esoteric was difficult to attract. Then came the Environmental Investigation Agency, an NGO based in the United Kingdom that, among other interests, specialises in undercover investigations to expose transnational wildlife crimes.

"We talked for many years about joint projects, and we certainly shared information, but a year and a half ago, the EIA secured funding from the UK Government's Department for Environment, Food and Rural Affairs. That was a game changer for them and for us in the area of properly being able to investigate the international illegal wildlife trade," Edwin says.

WFFT was awarded £20,000 to investigate the illicit trail in and around Thailand, including Laos, Vietnam, Cambodia and China. The Foundation has also dedicated another £10,000 of its own funds to the operation. Within the first three months, they discovered three tiger farms within Thailand that did not officially exist and found evidence there are links that reach well into the upper echelons of power. Equipment including a drone has been bought and WFFT has employed two investigators; a data gatherer who follows the threads and virtual trails on the internet, linking those involved in both the legal trade and the shadowy, illegal trade, and an undercover operative who is embedded in enemy territory. Edwin is also hands-on in some of the more dangerous investigations. They expect to have ample evidence for multiple papers and make a ground-breaking, field-shaking presentation on the investigation at the next CITES conference in Sri Lanka in 2019.

Edwin says his health challenges in addition to his mother's heart attack in 2017 and his father's strokes have given him the added impetus to ensure his Foundation is structured so that the work will continue long after he dies.

"I realise now that if tomorrow I am found to be very sick, I probably would say I wish I had a bit more time, but I've got the most out of it already," he says. "I feel that I have done something. If I were to find out I was dying, I would not wish I had climbed Mount Everest or done something else that is on a lot of people's bucket lists.

"There is nothing I want to do in my life that I have not done other than to have a bit more time to continue on with what I am doing. I am living that dream that people talk about, but it is my daily reality now. There is satisfaction and comfort in that."

Tommy concurs with this view. It is the day-to-day individual cases and the on-the-ground initiatives that offer deepest satisfaction in their work.

"I have been painting structures in the macaque field today. I will be very happy when I see some macaques moving out of quarantine and going in there," he says. "That, for me, is a personal achievement, to see an animal that we have rescued, who may not be necessarily have huge conservation value, move into an environment in which they can exhibit natural behaviours. That animal is entitled to be protected and cared for both in the wild and in captivity. It is the little things like that that give you a sense of gratitude and a sense of achievement that keep people like me going."

Noi says she also finds joy in getting outside, both physically and to talk to people outside the organisation. She says any lasting changes she is part of depends on a broader understanding of the need to care for wildlife and conserve habitats. More than that, she says there is a long way to go in changing attitudes in Thailand, and more broadly in Asia, about the place of animals.

"There are so many who still see them as something to eat, or something to make money from," she says. "There are still so many who do not care at all. There is still so much to do in education."

Tommy believes the future for wild animals is bleak, but while he says he is a realist, he tries not to get weighed down by his intimate knowledge of the environmental disasters to come.

"How do people like me who work in such an environment where we are doing our little bit to protect the wild animals of one nation continue to be inspired and fight for this? We rationalise it so we can live with it. But the sad reality is the world is fucked and so many animals are simply not going to make it," he says. "The orang-utans are going to be gone soon. It is real. Extinctions *will* occur. It *is* happening, not it *might*. I have to focus on the little things, the small parts that I can effect a change for. I have to or I would give up now and would go insane."

Research shows that 200 more primate species will be extinct by 2050. The reasons include poor global environmental management and internationally cohesive planning.

"For example, Thailand's 115 National Parks and protected areas are all marooned and surrounded by urban areas," Tommy says. "There are no corridors, so the animals that are protected will have to be controlled. Too many elephants in one area will kill the forest.

"We are almost at the point where wild places will not be truly wild anymore because they will all have to have some form of human controls and that is terrifying."

Animals are dramatically affected by climate change. They are very sensitive to a degree or two's difference and ecologists agree that the planet is in the grip of the sixth mass extermination on the earth: The Anthropocene or human-caused extinction.

Noi would like to see more Thai staff working in all facets of the Foundation, because she sees that as the key to broader understanding of wildlife management and care. There are many already on staff, but she wants that increased.

Noi says the raid on their rescue centre in 2012 was something of a wake-up call. She said she had not thought a great deal about the law before that, because it was rarely mentioned or acted on, but when faced with officials asking for documentation that she could not quickly access, reality hit home.

She has also developed a begrudging respect for the politics.

"At the beginning, I did not like authority or politics. I did not trust it. My father worked under the mayor when I was a child, and I recall he spent a lot of time away from the family. It seemed fake to me too, like everyone was pretending. I still do not like politics, but I see the importance of its ability to bring about change for the people."

Noi says life with Edwin is a series of endless worries.

"I always worry because many people do not like us," she says. "Edwin has a very big mouth and a loud voice. He is strong and says things straight and sometimes I wish he would shut his mouth. Thai people talk badly about the way he just says things and don't like that. It is not the Thai way."

Noi says in the years she has been with Edwin, her inner strength has grown. Once submissive and quiet, she has found her own voice and is less afraid to use it.

"I think I have changed to be the sort of person that if you hit me first, I will hit you back," she says. "I was not always like that."

Noi says she still worries that one day Edwin's agitation and outspoken-ness might have him thrown out of the country – or worse. She worries about having to go on without him. But the fear of that has lessened in recent years, as WFFT has expanded and Edwin's circles have come to include many people in powerful positions.

"I feel confident it would not happen now, or if they tried, there would be too much of a big fight afterwards," she says.

"We are stronger and his supporters are louder than they used to be. I think more people see the sense in what he does. He is not just someone who is trying to change everything and get attention; he is someone who is trying to change things to make them better for the animals and also Thailand itself."

Edwin's place at the parliamentary table has changed him for the better. He is still unapologetic about being a rule breaker and game changer, but he no longer sees compromise as weakness.

"I am not a small, fragile person with a softness who saves those poor animals. I am the absolute opposite. I am an arsehole who is a big, fat, ugly old man with a big voice who people think probably does this work to make himself famous. I am not that, or at least my motivation is far from that.

"In my plan, in the next two or three years, WFFT will double in size. When I die, I want people to look at old photos of me with Meow swimming and say 'that was the founder. He did something no one did before him. He started this'."

Because WFFT is so big now, Noi accepts that she must have help with bookkeeping and administration, but she struggles to trust others to do them properly. She says she is used to having everything under her watchful eye. She likes to keep tabs on the Foundation's expenses and even when other staff take on some of the work, she is not prepared to let it go entirely. And then there is travel, which in the last 12 months alone has included trips with Edwin to Laos, Holland, Australia and many shorter trips within Thailand.

"I am so very tired," she says. "I feel like the load is too much sometimes; the days are too long. There are so many pressures on me. Many of them are practical – things to do or places I must go – but there is also a great load of feelings too. I worry about Edwin and his health. I worry about his stress. He does not look after himself well enough, and he says sometimes it is my job, but he is difficult and does not accept help.

"I think this is just our life. This is just how it is."

Edwin will build a new house for him and Noi at the edge of Project 4 soon. He plans a simple structure with two bedrooms with open spaces and good airflow to offset the relentless Thai heat and humidity. It will be the first time since his incarnation as a wildlife warrior that he has not lived in a shared space, when he will be in neither apartment nor with staff at an adjoining wall.

"I hope that one day next year I might be able to sit on my balcony with a gin and tonic at five o'clock and just quietly watch the elephants and the gibbons," he says.

"I dream of that. I really want to be able to sit and enjoy what I have helped to bring about. I think that then I will be able to feel satisfied, to just look and think *we did all that for them*."